Write. Publish. Prosper.

How to Write Prolifically, Publish Globally, and Prosper Eternally

Other Titles by Connie Ragen Green

Living the Internet Lifestyle: Quit Your Job, Become an Entrepreneur, and Live Your Ideal Life

Huge Profits with a Tiny List: 50 Ways to use Relationship Marketing to Increase Your Bottom Line

The Weekend Marketer: Say Goodbye to the '9 to 5', Build an Online Business, and Live the Life You Love

Time Management Strategies for Entrepreneurs: How to Manage Your Time to Increase Your Bottom Line

The Inner Game of Internet Marketing

Membership Sites Made Simple: Start Your Own Membership Site for Passive Online Income

Article Marketing: How to Attract New Prospects, Create Products, and Increase Your Income

Targeted Traffic Techniques for Affiliate Marketers

Huge Profits with Affiliate Marketing: How to Build an Online Empire by Recommending What You Love

The Transformational Entrepreneur: Creating a Life of Dedication and Service

Write. Publish. Prosper.

How to Write Prolifically, Publish Globally, and Prosper Eternally

By
Connie Ragen Green

Copyright © 2015 by Hunter's Moon Publishing
ISBN Paperback: 978-1-937988-21-0
ISBN Kindle: 978-1-937988-20-3

Hunter's Moon Publishing
http://HuntersMoonPublishing.com

Interior Design by Geoff Hoff
Cover Design by Shawn Hansen

Dedication

Education is what remains after one has forgotten
what one has learned in school.
~ Albert Einstein

When I began teaching in the 1980s it was impossible for me to fathom just how strong a bond and connection would be formed between myself and the students I would teach over the years. During a twenty year period I came to know some of the most hard working an courageous people I would ever encounter. This included the parents, siblings, extended family members, and even the neighbors of the children who sat in my classroom.

Therefore, I am dedicating this book to all of the young people who were in my classrooms during my twenty years as a teacher, as well as the others I've mentioned above.

This was not an easy time to teach or to be a student in the public schools of Los Angeles, yet we managed to forge ahead each day and to accomplish great things together. These great things included the broad spectrum of academics, sports, technology, the arts, and life in general as well as in the specifics of day to day human interactions.

My goal was that the year you spent with me be a memorable one. That you would not simply grow one year older during that time, but to also see your world as an ever expanding universe filled with hope, joy, and endless opportunity.

So whether you were a Kindergartner, high school student, or somewhere in between when you were my student, thank you for teaching me life lessons that continue to help me navigate the waters of life and for sharing your true and unique self with me for a year. And thanks for helping me to stop taking myself so seriously. I can still hear your laughter as you learned that teachers are people, too.

And if our paths should cross again, as has already happened with so many of you on more occasions than I can count these days, know that I will forever be Mrs. Green, the teacher who gave you permission and even insisted you begin each day with a clean slate, and the person who still cares about you in a special and unconditional way.

Table of Contents

Foreword

Fulfilling the dream of seeing an idea you have come to life in the form of a published book never gets old. To date, I've published six books, and each time it feels as exciting as the first.

Every time you take an idea and turn it into a new book, you grow your business, your credibility, and your bottom line.

What you hold in your hands is Connie Ragen Green's eleventh published book, so if you've ever dreamed of writing one of your own, seeing it through to publication, and prospering from the doors that book will open for you, congratulations! You're on your way.

If you know Connie, she really needs no introduction, but for those of you who might not know her . . .

Let me tell you what I love about Connie Ragen Green: If she wants something, she goes after it, and she doesn't stop until she's captured it. Then, having successfully wrangled the thing, she steps out into the world and shares what she's learned with anyone who's serious about learning it, too.

That's tenacity. That's work ethic. That's success.

Anyone who dreams of writing and publishing a book can succeed in doing so – provided the individual gets the right guidance along the way. This book is that 'right guidance', and Connie Ragen Green will inspire you to reach your peak of tenacity and instill in you the kind of work ethic every successful author needs.

I know because she did it for me.

I met Connie in 2012 in what I consider to be a series of happy accidents that culminated in a right-place-at-the-right-time scenario for me.

Beginning in 2010, I'd been earning enough money with my writing to enable me to leave a 10-year college professorship and pursue writing full-time. By 2012, I'd sold over 1,000 short stories and published the first of my books to Amazon's Kindle platform. I felt I had a bright future, except for one thing: I had no idea how to grow my plateauing writing business. I knew *what* I needed to do, but I had no idea *how* to get it done.

Knowing I had to learn to market myself and create a powerful online presence led to that series of happy accidents, which included my attending my first-ever live marketing event and meeting Connie Ragen Green. During her presentation, she said something that resonated with me: "Do for a year what others won't, and you can live the rest of your life the way others can't."

I bought into it. Completely. I became a student of Connie's trainings, and what began as a chance meeting turned into a friendship. Listening to Connie's training, reading her books, and following her business model helped me overcome the plateau I'd reached in my writing business. To this day, I pay attention to what Connie pursues, and I listen when she has information to share.

Dig into this book, and take action. If you do, you'll be well on your way to writing, publishing, and prospering.

Shawn Hansen, Author Entrepreneur
http://ShawnHansen.com
January 8, 2015

Knowing the 'How-To' Strategy of the Game

When I first met the author of this book, Connie Ragen Green, she was negotiating the purchase of an upgraded seat across the aisle from me on a flight from Los Angeles to Amsterdam. She knew the rules of how to get an upgrade on board a flight, was courteous but forthright with the Dutch flight attendant, and got what she wanted.

In other words, she knew how to strategy of the game that those of us who fly tens or hundreds of thousands of miles a year choose to play.

Connie explained to me, after we landed in Amsterdam and were seated in one of the airport lounges awaiting divergent flights to other parts of Europe, how she came to author a number of books and establish a business of her own. It was a fascinating discussion.

As an MBA with an emphasis in entrepreneurship, I've interviewed hundreds of small business owners, consulted with over a hundred at various stages of their growth as part of an incubator and a Chamber of Commerce program I helped launch, and even taken an equity stake or temporary executive role approximately 25 companies. So I know what to look for—both the warning signs, which are legion, as well as the opportunities—when a business owner shares their experience and vision. Often within the first twenty minutes of conversation, I lose interest, because the flaws are almost insurmountable.

The discussion with Connie was one of those rare conversations on the other end of the spectrum: not only had she chosen a clearly defined vision, but she'd executed it with a laser focus that belied experience and success in previous ventures. Indeed, once we started talking about past careers, it was clear that her education and real estate experience were instrumental to informing the decisions she made in launching and growing her current business.

Readers might ask how their past experiences can be put to use to effect a successful online business. I don't have all the answers, nor, do I suspect, Connie does. But I think her success, as laid out in previous books, as well as the current tome you have before you, may help jumpstart a few ideas for how your past successes and failures—the latter being a more powerful tool than any success—can help you grow a successful online business.

Tim Siglin, Co-founder, Transitions, Inc.
A business and technology development firm
and Chairman, Braintrust Digital, Inc.

Preface

'Follow you passion. The rest will attend to itself. If I can do it, anybody can do it. It's possible. And it's your turn. So go for it. It's never too late to become what you always wanted to be in the first place.'
~ J. Michael Straczynski

I was the writer that didn't write. At least I didn't write very often. Please allow me to explain. Ever since I was a little girl of nine or ten I was in love with the idea of writing a book. I would tell this to everyone I met and they would encourage me to write something and show it to them. I wrote a few poems and then decided short stories would be better. Eventually I decided that I wanted to write for film and television. This passion continued through high school and into college, where I took several courses on creative writing, screenwriting, and persuasive writing.

Then in my early twenties I returned to short story writing, with a new genre known as 'flash fiction', 'micro fiction', 'postcard fiction', 'sudden fiction', or 'very short stories'. Whereas the typical short story would have fewer than seventy-five hundred words, these shorter ones could have as few as three hundred words. In China these stories are referred to frequently as a 'smoke long' or 'palm-sized' story, with the comparison being that the story should be finished before the reader could finish smoking a cigarette. My thinking was that I could write something quickly and still be considered an author.

Write. Publish. Prosper.

It wasn't that I didn't write at all; it was more like I only wrote when I had to. I would wait until the last minute to write a paper or a story, pour my heart and soul into in, and then rest on my laurels until the next assignment was due.

After college my writing became even more sporadic. Sometimes a year or longer would pass before I would write even a ten page short story.

During the summer of 1984 I had a job at a production company in Los Angeles where I did a variety of jobs assisting producers, directors, and writers with what they were doing for the major studios. That is where I met a man named J. Michael Straczynski, an up and coming young writer. We were just about the same age and I would share my ideas with him for stories I wanted to write for television and film.

Joe, as he preferred to be called, had written a spec script. This is also known as a speculative screenplay, which is a non-commissioned, unsolicited screenplay. These are typically written by a screenwriter who hopes to have the script optioned and eventually purchased by a producer, production company, or studio. What he wrote was a spec script for a television show called *He-Man and the Masters of the Universe*.

This show debuted through something referred to as 'barter syndication' in September 1983, and became the first syndicated show to be based on a toy. The producers loved his script and hired him as a staff writer. This is a big deal, and Joe was smart enough to understand this.

One day I was sharing another one of my ideas with him, explaining what each character might say and do and how the scene would begin and end. He stretched out his arm at a ninety degree angle with his palm wide open, directly in front of my face to stop me from talking. I will never forget what he then said to me:

"Don't tell me any more stories. Write your stories down and I will read them."

I didn't do that. The rest is history. Joe went on to become the executive story editor for the new *Twilight Zone*, executive producer for *Murder, She Wrote*, and created a series called *Babylon 5*, for which he wrote ninety-two of its one hundred ten episodes. Over the years since I knew him he's won a plethora of awards, including Emmy Awards and Hugo Awards and the Ray Bradbury Award for Outstanding Dramatic Presentation for his series *Babylon 5*. He went forward with his dream of being a writer and I gave up my dream.

During the next twenty years or so I did do some writing. I wrote about a dozen short stories and two screenplays. I refused to edit or rewrite any of my writing, so once they were written I was finished. One Christmas I printed about a dozen copies of my first draft screenplay, tied red ribbon around each of them, and gave them out as Christmas presents to my family and close friends. They weren't sure what to say to me, so they just said 'thank you'.

Fast forward to 2006, my first full year working as an online entrepreneur. I realized pretty quickly that writing would be crucial to my success, so I began blogging and finally writing short articles to submit to the directories. The writing was mediocre at best but I kept at it. Soon I could write a three hundred word blog post or article in less than an hour.

In Joe's quote at the beginning of this section he emphasized the importance of following your passion. Passion is an interesting concept. If you follow it blindly you risk falling into the abyss of the 'starving artist'. If you follow your passion strategically, however, you will find that it serves you well in every area of your life. It's your choice, of course.

Even though I came very late to the 'published author' party I am reaping the benefits in a way I could never have previously imagined. And that's exactly why I felt compelled to write and publish this book.

With ten books under my belt within the past four and a half years, as well as compiling half a dozen others on the topics of success and entrepreneurship and contributing to more than a dozen other books on similar topics, it was time for me to open the vault and expose the secrets to my writing and publishing success. That is how and why this book has come to be, and I sincerely hope it will lead you down a path of joyous prosperity as these concepts, strategies, and techniques have for me and so many others. I'd like to think Joe would approve of this strategy.

Connie Ragen Green
Santa Barbara, California
January 12, 2015

Acknowledgements

No one who achieves success does so without
acknowledging the help of others.
The wise and confident acknowledge
this help with gratitude.
~ Alfred North Whitehead

I firmly believe that books do not come into existence through only the sole writing efforts of the author. Many people play crucial roles in the creative process, beginning with a friend or colleague with whom you have a brief conversation that leads to an idea for a book and ending with the completed book being available for sale and distributed around the world.

In this case I wish to thank my Platinum Mastermind members - Adrienne Dupree, Debbie O'Grady, Maria Lassila, Kimberly Schramm, Suzanne Ascioti, Ed Manske, Tom Armstrong, Lauren Slade, Jack Marriott, Judy Mick, Joyce Jagger, Cynthia Charleen Alexander, Mike Darling, Kit Rosato, Leslie Cardinal, and Ben Oyortey – for always pushing me to share more of my writing and marketing strategies with them as a way to build their own businesses. Our group makes us all stronger.

My family, both immediate and extended, also deserves to be acknowledged. Thank you for your silent support while I am working on a project and your not so silent exuberance when the project comes to fruition. I love each of you for who you are!

Write. Publish. Prosper.

Books don't format themselves and covers do not magically appear, so thanks to Geoff Hoff and Shawn Hansen for making my thoughts and ideas presentable to the world.

Also, a huge thanks of gratitude to my email subscribers. You are a part of my life every day and I want to thank and acknowledge you for keeping me on my toes with every email I write, blog post I publish, and podcast I release.

May you all write prolifically, publish globally, and prosper for eternity!

Introduction

The supreme accomplishment is to blur the line
between work and play.
~ Arnold J. Toynbee

Anyone can write and publish a book in about four to six weeks. I know because I have now done it successfully eleven times since releasing my first book, *Huge Profits with a Tiny List: 50 Way to use Relationship Marketing to Increase Your Bottom Line* in the summer of 2010. So if you are thinking this is a dramatic claim, know that I have tested out and proven the process I am teaching here both personally and with my high level mentoring students. And I'm not talking about a flimsy, pamphlet type book, but instead a full length manuscript of approximately twenty to thirty thousand words.

This book comes in at almost forty thousand words, in part because I am an overachiever and partially because I asked two of my colleagues, Dennis Becker and Tim Siglin to share their thoughts on the writing process with you in Appendix A at the end of the book. I also included an entire seven day e-course and one of my most popular and recent Special Reports in Appendix B. These two appendices added roughly ten thousand words to the book, half of which were repurpose and the other half written by others. Feel free to borrow this strategy if it suits your needs.

It was inevitable that I would write a book on this topic, and when I finally decided to do this my first thought was that

I would be teaching the exact model as I use in my own business. What an honor it is to share my own example as a Case Study for you to study, emulate, and then tweak to match your own style. What ended up happening was that in the writing of this book I further refined my process to help you even more with everything that is required to build a business based around your book and its topic.

The idea of writing, publishing, and then building a rewarding and prosperous lifestyle around your topic is not a new one. At least since the 1950s, that I am aware of, it has been the goal of thought leaders to share their thoughts, ideas, and experiences with others through a book, and to then take this on the road with a book tour, interviews, live presentations, and sometimes a coaching program.

What is different in the 2010s is the idea that you can write about any topic, regardless of your background; self-publish, thereby cutting out the traditional publisher as the middleman, and build a lucrative online business based on what you have written about your niche topic.

At least eighty percent of the population would like to write a book, yet fewer than ten percent ever do so. I was one of these statistics during most of my adult life, until I developed this process and fine tuned it to work for any non-fiction topic. If you are a writer of fiction works, my guess is that you could also make this system work for you with a few small tweaks.

Anyone can write and publish a book on their niche topic, lay a foundation based upon the book, and create a prosperous business that can change their life forever within about four to six weeks. I know this to be true after doing it myself and having dozens of my own students do it as well.

This is my honest belief and the Thesis Statement upon which this book is based. Now a belief is simply a thought you keep thinking, so it is my goal to turn this into a core belief for you as well.

Many books have been written on the topic of how to write and publish a book, yet seldom do I find them to include the step by step details of how to include your book as a part of your overall platform in which you can build and grow a prosperous business. That is my intention here, and one that will make a difference for you right now, in the coming weeks and months, and for the remainder of your life if you allow what I am teaching to wash over you in a way that permeates your thinking.

My goal in this Introduction is to gently introduce the material that is covered in this book. I want to set the stage for you as the reader, and prepare you for what can be expected from reading this book through to the end. Hopefully, my description of each Section I have included here will grab your attention and intensify your desire to find out more about this topic and make you want to devour the concepts and put them into action for your own good. This is exactly what will be revealed if you continue reading:

In the first Section – *Why Do You Want to Write, Publish, and Prosper?* – I cover the topics of building credibility and authority and how to change your life and the lives of others around you. Here is where you will be introduced to the three-pronged approach of writing a book while blogging and podcasting. I also share my experiences with volunteering, charitable organizations, and non-profits. Finally, I cover what it means to leave a legacy based on your body of work

Section Two, *What Does it Mean to Write, Publish, and Prosper?*, introduces the idea of having a multiple streams philosophy when it comes to earning income and also the concept of shaping the way others perceive you and what you have to offer the world.

What If You Write, Publish, and Prosper? is the focus of Section Three, and here is where I share my thoughts and experiences on how to best reach the world with your message, using storytelling to flesh out your business, and learning how to live the life you love and deserve.

The fourth section of this book gets into the meat of the matter by answering the question *What Is The Step By Step Process Of Writing, Publishing, And Prospering?* Here is where I cover planning, researching, and pre-writing for your book, creating your outline, advanced writing and creating strategies, and how to actually make sure your book gets written.

Section Five discusses *What's Next in the Process?* And talks about publishing, marketing, public speaking, live events, mentoring, consulting, and beyond and taking it all to the next level in your journey to build a lucrative business based on your book or books.

After all that I have learned through writing my previous books and contributing to many other people's books over the past five years, it was inevitable that I would finally write a book on exactly how you can emulate this as a business model as well.

Have I properly whetted your appetite for what is to come? I certainly hope so, and actually can't wait to learn from you how you have used my teachings to write and publish your own book and lay the foundation for a business based on what you have written. I also want to hear from you about any tweaks or modifications you may have made to suit your own needs and goals. And, most importantly, I want to know how your life has changed since becoming a published author.

Section One
Why Do You Want To Write, Publish, And Prosper?

Chapter 1

Building Authority and Credibility

Communication is a skill that you can learn, like riding a bike or typing. If you're willing to work at it, you can rapidly improve the quality of every part of your life.
~ Brian Tracy

No one told me that writing a book would change my life so dramatically. I had hoped it would help me grow my business, while also fulfilling a lifelong dream, but I could never have imagined what actually occurred in my life immediately following the publication of my first book, *Huge Profits with a Tiny List: 50 Ways to use Relationship Marketing to Increase Your Bottom Line* in July of 2010. What has transpired in my life since that time, both personally and professionally, has been nothing short of miraculous.

Immediately following the release of my book during that summer of 2010 I was asked to speak at several prestigious marketing conferences, including one hosted by online marketing legend Armand Morin. People followed me around, hung on my every word while I was speaking on stage, and readily purchased my products and programs at the end of my presentation. I was on fire and it felt wonderful.

This continued into the fall, and I could see that I had transformed from someone who was still putting the pieces together into someone others looked to for advice and for solutions to the problems they were facing as an online entrepreneur. I was once again a teacher and enjoyed this very much. I will never forget how it felt to go from where I was before my book came out to where I was able to go afterward. The doors of opportunity just kept opening for me, and then my business took off in a huge way.

What I am teaching and explaining in a detailed, step by step format in this book will help you to build your authority and credibility in your field very quickly. Unlike the corporate world, where you need extensive formal education and must sometimes work for decades in order to achieve such status, becoming a published author will fast track your success and take you to the top quickly, many times in just a matter of months.

What I am describing here has been done by many others before me. People such as Robert Kiyosaki, Tim Ferriss, Seth Godin, Suze Orman, Guy Kawasaki, Joel Fuhrman, Michael Hyatt, Bill Phillips, Dr. John Gray, and Michael Breus have done this over the past decade, building an entire career based on having a book and a platform to stake their claim as an credible expert and authority who had something special and important to share with the world. You can do exactly the same in your niche. If you are not yet familiar with some of the names I have mentioned here, take some time to Google them to see what they have achieved.

One of the people I named here is health and fitness expert Bill Phillips. I first met Bill in 2007, while attending a small group Mastermind in Palm Springs, California. As he sauntered on to the small platform in front of our group of about fifty people, my thought was that he was arrogant, opinionated, and unable to understand what it was like for someone like me to get into good physical shape and maintain that during my lifetime.

After Bill spoke for a few minutes I realized that I was totally incorrect in my initial impression of who he was. Here was a true expert in his niche, sharing his personal experiences as well as the research he was going into how the human body achieves and maintains optimal health and fitness.

Now Bill and I have become better acquainted, having spoken at the same event twice during the past several years and as a result of having attended his 'Fit For Life' fitness and nutrition camp in Golden, Colorado on two separate occasions during 2014.

Another person in my list is Dr. John Gray, author of more than twenty bestselling books, including his first one, *Men Are From Mars, Women Are From Venus.* I've shared the stage with John twice, speaking to groups of authors on the topic of positioning yourself as an authority and expert in your field.

This first book of his, the one I just mentioned, has sold more than fifty million copies and spent one hundred twenty-one weeks on the New York Times bestseller list. According to CNN it was the highest ranked work of non-fiction during the 1990s.

Gray is a relationship counselor turned speaker who started out like many other psychologists. In order to make a name for himself and stand out from the crowd he came up with a catchy idea related to his field of specialization and ran with it. I am in no way discounting his talent, skill, and ability in his field, but instead pointing out how he turned a career into an opportunity for entrepreneurship.

Instead of waiting for the world to find out what he had to offer, he moved forward with a passion and desire to share his message with those who were interested in knowing more about the differences between men and women and how that was related with interpersonal relationships.

Now you may be thinking that you are not an expert, and that other people are better suited to present the information you know on your topic. I would vehemently disagree with this line of thinking. You are an expert by virtue of the fact that you have information to share and are willing to share it.

Think about an expert you are familiar with on any topic. Let's just say it is a medical doctor with a specialization in a specific area of medicine. On what day did they become an expert? Was it the day they finished medical school, or when they finished the advanced study of their specialty, or when they began to work with patients, or when something else occurred? I believe they became an expert the day they believed they had important and specialized information they wanted to convey to others and began sharing this information in a variety of ways, culminating with their book being published.

We have now entered the age of specialization, so commit to becoming a specialist instead of a generalist on your topic. Does this make sense to you?

Much of this comes down to what the 'little voice' inside of your head is telling you on a regular basis. In Dr. Brian Alman's book, *The Voice: Overcome Negative Self-Talk and Discover Your Inner Wisdom* he explains how you can eliminate the negative chatter in your head and start listening to your inner wisdom. This is where the genius in you resides and can make all of the difference when you are seeking to change your life and be perceived as an expert and authority in your field.

Tapping into this unconscious potential, something we all have from the time we are born is the process of finding your voice. I have taught this concept since first coming online in 2006 and used it to turn myself into a writer and an online marketing strategist. Start out slowly, by telling yourself positive things throughout the day that will enable you to feel good about the work you are doing and the life you are living. Over time this will become specific affirmations such as 'I am learning more and more about my topic every single day and enjoy sharing this information with others.'

We tend to beat ourselves up regarding the events of our day to day life much more than we would admit. I first realized that I was doing this when I left my teaching position and stopped taking real estate clients. Each morning I would get out of bed, and instead of feeling excited about the possibilities of becoming an online entrepreneur and being ready to tackle the challenges and enjoy the rewards I was starting my negative self-talk before I reached the bathroom.

Within ten minutes of arising I had already 'voiced' all of the reasons I would not succeed that day. This went on for months before I brought it to an abrupt end. Once I turned that around and only voiced positive thoughts and ideas to myself each morning, my business began to take off and I finally came to understand the power we have when we talk to ourselves. This takes true courage to discover who we truly are on the inside and why it is so important for us to share ourselves with the world.

Dr. Alman teaches that we need to accept ourselves the way we are so that we can begin the process of hearing the little voice inside our head that holds our inner wisdom.

Blair Singer, motivational speaker and author of *Little Voice Mastery: How to Win the War Between Your Ears in 30 Seconds or Less and Have an Extraordinary Life!* divides the world into two distinct groups of people; the unconscious and the conscious. He describes the unconscious as those people who believe that they are simply passive beings in a world where others do things to them and cause them to have or to not have the things they want in their lives. The conscious people have mastered the ability to step outside of themselves and acknowledge that they are the 'cause', and not simply the 'effect' of someone else's actions by seeing things objectively.

I call this taking responsibility, and my journey towards becoming a more 'conscious' human being began at age fifty when my life changed as a result of my choice to leave my previous life behind and begin anew. Overnight I went from a life of working as an employee of the school district and a small business owner in real estate brokerage and appraisal to one of being the creative force in my new business venture as an online entrepreneur. It was both exhilarating and frightening, yet I was determined to be successful and do whatever it would take to make that happen.

Commit to walking down this path to becoming an authority and expert on your topic starting right now. It all starts with laying your foundation. I'll be discussing this in much greater detail later on in this book, but for now suffice it to say that you must get your name and your message out to the world in a big way. This begins with a three-pronged approach that includes setting up and posting regularly to a blog, writing a book, and designing a podcast series. All three – the blog, the book, and the podcast – will be created with the idea of giving you a platform in which to discuss your thoughts and ideas on your niche topic. I'll be teaching you exactly how to write and publish your book, so let's discuss your blog and podcast right here and now so that you can begin to develop a vision as to what this will look like for your business.

Blogging and Podcasting To Build Authority

The word *author* is derived from the word *authority*, and it is still true today that people who write books are considered to be authorities on their topic.

Like more than eighty percent of the population, I had always wanted to write a book, but had no idea what I would write about or how to get my ideas organized into a book format. After starting and stopping several times, I decided in the fall of 2005 that blogging would be the best way for me to get started down this path of writing on a regular basis and finding my voice when it came to my niche topic.

A blog consists of a series of posts, typically several hundred words in length that share information on your topic with your readers. They are arranged in reverse chronological order, meaning that your most recent posts will appear at the top of your site. I started out on a blogging platform called Typepad, because WordPress was simply too technologically daunting at that time, but switched over to the WordPress platform by 2008. This is now the standard for blogs and websites in general, predominantly due to the ease of use and flexibility with themes and plugins.

During my first year working online I started a dozen blogs, ranging in topics from health and fitness, small dogs, buying and selling real estate, reinventing your life, and writing eBooks. Within a few months I was exhausted from attempting to keep them all going, and decided to eliminate a few, spend more time on others, and focus most intently on the one on writing and marketing eBooks. That blog, EbookWritingandMarketingSecrets.com, became the basis for what is now my main site, ConnieRagenGreen.com.

Blogging and writing articles helped to turn me into a writer during 2006, and my writing improved over time. It became better in small increments at first, and now I can hold my own with professional writers who are much more organized and savvy than I am when it comes to this part of my life. Even though I had taught several hundred students, ranging in age from five to young adult, how to write and edit, it did not mean that I had been doing much of my own writing during that twenty year period. I wrote about this in the Preface to this book and I would encourage you to reread that section for emphasis to what I am writing here in this chapter.

It is believed that it takes somewhere between twenty-one and thirty consecutive days to form a habit, so when I challenged myself to write one hundred articles in one hundred days back then that was my attempt at getting into a writing habit for good. I did not achieve my goal of writing those hundred articles in a hundred days; it only took me seventy-eight days!

Teleseminars became a staple in my business at the end of 2006, and I hosted one every single week for a period of eighteen months. This experience served as the impetus and logical transition to hosting two podcast series a few years later. One of my podcasts was named as one of the top one hundred small business podcasts in 2014, an honor I am quite proud of and one that motivates me to work even harder in this area.

Whereas blogging allows visitors the opportunity to read what you are sharing, podcasts allow them to not only hear your words but to also experience the tone and demeanor of your voice. It is human nature for us to judge others by their words, so let people read your thoughts and ideas as well as hear you as soon as possible in your own business.

Podcasting is also finally being recognized in mainstream media and in influential magazines. By the spring of 2015 half of the new cars rolling off the assembly lines will have Internet connectivity; and within five to seven years it is estimated that this feature will be available in all new cars and as an add-on to older models. When that happens and there are podcasts available in everyone's car, it's not simply podcasts anymore; it's mainstream radio. This will level the playing field in business even further, and you can expect podcasts to become even more popular as a way to get your message out to the world, all while growing your business. You'll be able to reach those who are interested in your topic on a global level, regardless of whether or not they use a smart phone or have any experience with technology.

If you think about it, both blogging and podcasting are perfect vehicles for putting together your ideas and then creating the content for your book. In fact, my first book came from fifty articles I had posted to my blog over time during 2009 and then published in 2010. I then went on to record my thoughts on each of these in 2011 to launch my podcast series. I highly recommend and encourage you to do the same thing.

Begin With the End in Mind

So as you begin this process of writing a book and laying the foundation for a lucrative online business, begin with the end in mind as to how you want to set everything up. We will be discussing in great detail how you want to be perceived by others, the changes you will be able to make to your own life and the lives of others, how and why to share your message with the world, and exactly how you can live the life you love and deserve.

Later on in this book I will go into greater detail about how to create information products based on your book and its topic, but for now I will just share that being able to earn money while you are sleeping, travelling, or on vacation is an excellent business model.

Having a Vision and a Mission for your life will change everything you say, write, and do forever. Let's move on now in this journey to write prolifically, publish globally, and prosper eternally.

Chapter 2

Change Your Life and
the Lives of Others

*The changes in our life must come from the
impossibility to live otherwise than according
to the demands of our conscience;
not from our mental resolution
to try a new form of life.*
~ Leo Tolstoy

You may not be able to fully comprehend this idea fully right now, but you will be able to change your own life and the lives of people around you by following the concepts and ideas I am sharing with you in this book. This requires a leap of faith on your part, one that will pay off handsomely over time.

What I mean by this is that becoming a published author opens doors for you that you cannot yet imagine. Increased opportunities lead to a significant increase in income, and this can be the key to you building a future for yourself and your family that would otherwise not have been possible.

I describe the life I created for myself up until age fifty as being one of mediocrity. I guess you could say I had given up on having the life I dreamed of, and probably couldn't have verbalized what that life would be like even if someone had offered to grant it as a wish back in those days. Instead, my day to day existence was something I tolerated, until it just became unbearable for me.

Often I am asked why some people succeed in life and others continue to just go through the paces each day, and it is my firm belief that we do not initiate a major change in our current circumstances until the pain of not doing so is simply too great for us to bear.

Now I did not write my first book right away; it was four years between the time I started my online business and published that first book. Why?

It wasn't because I did not want to. It wasn't because I felt like I didn't have anything worthwhile to say. It was because I wasn't sure how to get started, and that's why I am teaching the process here.

But let's get back to how you can change your life and the lives of the people around you by becoming a published author.

The book is your first step towards creating and building an information products business that will provide you with the time and financial freedom to live the life you choose.

Whether you are currently employed by a company, have your own business, or work from home, most likely you have experienced the feeling of not having enough hours in the day or dollars in the bank. I was trading time for money in an endless merry-go-round that never put me ahead of the curve. This was my day to day reality as well, and I did not know how to break out of the vicious cycle of feeling guilty when I spent money I truly didn't have or took time off work because I would not be earning money during that time either.

The result was that I worked for over three hundred days each year for over twenty years, missed almost every special occasion with family and friends, was not able to see one of my extended family members be sworn in as a United States citizen, and still had no extra time or money when all was said and done.

When I made the conscious decision to leave my old life behind and reinvent myself in 2005, the desire to spend more time with my family and friends and to have the money to do more in my life was the powerful 'reason why' that motivated me to move forward.

Volunteering with Charities and Non-Profits

In the late fall of 2005 I had lunch with a long time friend named Mary Lynn. We chose a vegan restaurant that was new to the area, and as we waited for the server to take our order I began telling her about my new business on the Internet and that I would be moving to Santa Clarita, a desert community about twenty miles north of where we both lived presently, which was in the San Fernando Valley section of Los Angeles.

I began to share how I was going to start volunteering for charitable organizations and to help them to raise more money for the causes they were involved with. Mary Lynn allowed me to go on for several minutes before stopping me to ask,

"Do you actually know anything about fundraising, Connie?"

The server came and took our order and then, without skipping a beat, I continued to tell her my plans. I said that no, I had never done anything like this before in my life, but that I knew there were people already involved with charities and non-profits that would teach me what to do and would be happy to have me help them. Fast forward ten years and I have helped to raise more than a half million dollars for a variety of charitable organizations and love every minute of it. The power of intention and inspired action can move mountains, and I want you to know that you can achieve any and all goals you set for yourself.

Within three months of this lunch and conversation with my friend I had moved into my new home in Santa Clarita and was ready to start volunteering. Because I had no idea where to begin (no one in my former life was involved in this way) I turned to Google for the information I was seeking. I Googled 'volunteering in Santa Clarita' to see what would come up and there on the first page was something about the Rotary Club of Santa Clarita.

Over my lifetime I had driven through cities and towns that showed the Rotary wheel as you entered the city limits, but I had never known anyone who shared with me that they were a member. I went to Rotary.org and discovered that this is an international service organization with clubs in more than two hundred countries around the world.

There are more than thirty thousand clubs with about 1.2 million members, and some notable Rotarians include twenty-ninth United States President Warren G. Harding, Finnish composer Jean Sibelius, German novelist and Nobel laureate Thomas Mann, and JC Penney founder James Cash Penney.

Rotary was started in 1905 by Chicago attorney Paul Harris, as a place where professionals with diverse backgrounds could exchange ideas and form meaningful, lifelong friendships. One of their first projects was to construct a public restroom outside of City Hall, much to the dismay of local shopkeepers and saloon owners. Today Rotary's biggest projects include installing clean water wells in third world nations and to help the World Health Organization and others to eradicate polio from our planet. Lofty goals, but ones that will change our world forever.

I allowed myself to be intimidated by the idea that the current Rotarians in Santa Clarita would not be open to meeting me, but I finally mustered the courage to show up at a meeting in July of 2006. There were about fifty members and guests present that day, and among them were my new veterinarian and dentist, a psychotherapist I had listened to on the local radio station, the owners of that radio station, as well as the Mayor and two councilman. When they asked me to introduce myself I reluctantly took the microphone and mumbled something about being a real estate appraiser and broker. The truth was that I had no real business at that moment, having resigned from the school district weeks earlier and having given away my real estate clients over the previous months.

I continued to attend meetings every couple of weeks or so and in November of that year someone asked me if I'd like to apply for membership. In December I was inducted into the Club and into Rotary International and my life of dedication to service had officially begun.

This year we have our first Chinese president, Gary C.K. Huang. In 2008 I was fortunate enough to visit the Rotary Club in Beijing, China with three other Rotarians from southern California. I have also spent time in Bangkok, Thailand with Rotary and almost every year for the past six years I have visited the Rotary Club in the small town in Finland when I am there to see my family that lives there full time.

Since that time I have joined several other organizations and cannot imagine my life without volunteering and helping others, many of whom live halfway around the world and I will never meet face to face. I've now spent time volunteering in the United States, as well as spending time in China, Mexico, and Thailand representing Rotary.

Helping others less fortunate is an excellent way to focus your attention on what is truly important in your life. I dare you to think about your own troubles when you are doing something to help someone else who is truly in need. I've worked with families dealing with domestic violence, severely disabled children, and people who simply do not have enough food to eat every day. It has humbled me to come full circle in this way, as I grew up in poverty and know what it's like to go to bed hungry.

Leaving a Legacy

Writing a book and building a business around your topic enable you to leave a legacy to those who care about most in your life. I was not even familiar with this concept until I had been working online for a couple of years. Without going into too many personal details, I will share that my family will be taken care of for generations to come because of what I have set up online. That is a feeling you have to experience to understand fully and one that gives opportunities to family members who will arrive long after we are gone.

Another part of creating a legacy is to give your family something to be proud of and to aspire to in their lives. I know for a fact that my family members are more motivated and inspired than ever before to do their best and to reach for higher and higher achievements and goals in their daily lives. This makes me so proud of them and grateful that our lives have taken this turn.

As you can see, leaving a legacy is about so much more than money. It's about empowering those around you with encouragement, purpose, and love. By striving to be the best you can be every day you inspire excellence in others. You also serve as a role model for your family, your friends and even your colleagues. You can strive to be the one person living in pursuit of excellence that raises the standards and the behaviors of everyone around them. Your life is your greatest legacy, and following the teachings in this book makes it possible for you to do more than you ever thought possible or imagined.

We all want to feel that we have a purpose beyond ourselves. To leave a legacy of purpose, I believe you must make your life about something much bigger than you. We are not going to live forever, but we can live on through the legacy we leave and the positive impact we make in the world through our body of work and our actions.

You can have a positive impact on people today, and years from today. Perhaps they will contact you, as people are now doing with me, to let you know that you encouraged them to move forward with something they always wanted to do. That is indeed a wonderful legacy.

We all leave a legacy when we are gone, whether we have planned it consciously or not. What will your legacy be?

I sincerely hope that you can now see how what I am proposing here will change your life and the lives of those around you.

Section Two
What Does It Mean To Write, Publish, And Prosper?

Chapter 3

Multiple Streams of Online Income

*Money won't create success;
the freedom to make it will.
~ Nelson Mandela*

An interesting thing happened in my life the year I became a school teacher. It was 1986 and the political climate in the United States was changing rapidly. Without boring you too much with the gory details, suffice it to say that teachers, for the most part, were not looked upon favorably in our society during that time. They were perceived as greedy, uncaring individuals who had little interest in children or education. I wanted to become a teacher to help educate the poorest, most underprivileged children in Los Angeles, so I was jumping into the fray knowingly. What I did not expect was to become a part of an ongoing struggle between the school district, the administration, and the teachers' unions.

This led to me maintaining my real estate appraisal and broker licenses and certifications and keeping my business open, so as to have an additional way to earn income if necessary. This ended up being an excellent idea, even though I could not have predicted what was to come during my first year of teaching.

When I received my credential and was assigned to a fifth and sixth grade combination class, I was in heaven. Children aged ten to twelve quickly became my favorite ones to teach, and I went on to teach this age group for fourteen of my twenty years as an educator. My intention at the beginning of that school year was to phase out my real estate career and devote my working life to teaching in the classroom.

But the teacher's in the Los Angeles School District were already uneasy about pay, working conditions, and insurance coverage before I arrived. Within a few weeks the union announced that we would be going through a variety of work slowdown and stoppage phases during the school year, and that if our demands were not met we would take the ultimate work action by going out on strike.

If was a long school year, one where I had to do a dance to please everyone involved and still maintain my integrity, and we did walk out before that school year was over. At that moment everything I knew and believed about earning income and supporting myself went out the window and I began searching for a new paradigm. You could say that my desire to have the business I have today began more than twenty-five years ago as I walked the picket line in front of my elementary school each day during the strike.

My actions made me unemployed and uninsured in an instant, and I began to stand up for my rights and the rights of my students in a way that was unrecognizable to anyone who had known me previously. I was a force to be reckoned with when it came to what I believed. You could say that at the age of thirty-one I finally became an adult.

Now you may be wondering what this has to do with writing a book and creating an online empire. The answer is that it has everything to do with it. If you have ever been put into a situation where your life is turned upside down, or if, as I did back then, you put yourself in this type of situation, then you know that your survival instincts kick in and all bets are off as to the actions you will take to protect yourself, your beliefs and values, and those whom you love.

When faced with financial ruin I took the only route that made sense to me at the time; I was a striking teacher by morning and a real estate professional by afternoon. Right then and there I made the decision to stay in real estate and to never put myself in a position of only having one way to earn a living.

Because I would be losing the income from teaching during the time we were on strike, I took a proactive approach to increasing my income from real estate right away. Instead of waiting for clients to come to me to buy or sell property, I explored the rental market to see what could be done there. I then placed a small classified advertisement in the local newspaper for one of our desirable, yet affordable rental units. Several people called the day the ad came out and I told them all to meet me in the parking lot of my real estate office on Saturday morning at ten.

We all met that Saturday and then caravanned over to see the townhome that was available as a rental. One couple decided it was perfect for them and filled out an application right there on the kitchen table. Within three days they had signed the lease and I had received a commission check for one half of the first month's rent. It was the easiest income I had ever earned since starting my real estate endeavors and I continued to do this every Saturday until I had more clients and deals in the pipeline. Out of adversity had come triumph, and I wanted more of this.

I yearned for the freedom to earn money in my own time and space. My 'multiple streams of income' mindset was born on that day and it basically took me more than twenty years to put it all into place in a way that worked best for my goals and dreams. As Nelson Mandela said in the quote I used at the beginning of this chapter, money doesn't create success, but the freedom to make it will. If this sounds like something you want to be a part of, then continue to read on as I unfold the details of how to make it happen.

The Multiple Streams Plan

Writing a book is the first step in the plan to create multiple streams of income. The next steps include setting up your online presence, building a list, and creating a funnel.

In *Chapter One* I began the discussion of having a blog and a podcast as a way to have an online presence and help you to get your book written and launched. This refers to a hosted WordPress blog (see the *Resources* section at the end of this book for more information) and to a podcast you will launch over at iTunes.

Let me say here that none of what I am recommending in this book is easy. It takes hard work and dedication that most people are not willing to do for the duration. Instead of being like most people, use this challenge as an opportunity to stand out from the crowd and be acknowledged for what you have to offer the world. It will be worth the sacrifices now to build a future that will be so enlightening, meaningful, and worthwhile, I promise. And always remember my motto:

'Do for a year what others won't;
Live forever the way other can't.'

Most of us never dreamed we would be blogging regularly, podcasting our thoughts and ideas to the world, and writing books that would help others to change their lives. These activities were not included in the job description of any work we have done in the past, yet they are the ones that are required to create multiple streams of online income. So congratulate yourself in advance for the journey you are about to undertake, and know that the rewards will far outweigh the sacrifices.

I will take time here to say a little about the technology that will be required with the business I am teaching you here. Not being very technical myself, I've always had someone to help me in this area. I now have several people who do various things at different times in the areas of technology I need.

My recommendation is to have two people who can help you with this. People who trade time for money are sometimes not as available or reliable as we would like for them to be, so do not leave yourself open to having any down time in your business because of a technological issue. Because many people are offering their services to do this type of work, hourly rates are still relatively inexpensive and will be affordable for you.

Once you have set up your blog and hosted your first podcast you are ready to set up a marketing funnel that will enable you to build a list of people who are interested in you and what you have to say on your topic, and to then begin earning some income with your own products and appropriate products from others. This will all be a part of the funnel I will now describe and explain in an introductory way; we go into much greater depth and detail on this part of the process in *Chapter 11*.

Your Marketing Funnel

Think about the last time you visited someone's blog or website. More than likely they offered you at least one way to leave your name and email address so that they could stay in touch with you. If you agreed and signed up, then you became a part of their 'permission based' list and received emails from them with some regularity. Visit my two sites to see what I mean:

http://ConnieRagenGreen.com
http://HugeProfitsTinyList.com

In each case you can see that I make it simple for you to stay in touch with me. When you type in your first name and primary email address you are simultaneously taken to a thank you page and added to my autoresponder service (more on this later) to begin receiving my email messages.

You were promised a free giveaway when you opted in to my list, and that can be delivered on the thank you page, within the first email message, or both. The free giveaway, typically a short report or an audio recording becomes the first piece of your funnel.

You can also create an e-course, which is simply a series of five or seven short emails that teach your prospect something about your topic. I have included an example of an e-course later in this book.

Based on the response you get to your free giveaway and e-course you will go on to create a simple product based upon your topic. You'll want this product to be 'evergreen', meaning that the information contained in it will be good for years to come.

Additional products follow, and these are completely digital as well, meaning that they will sell while you are sleeping, on vacation, and doing something completely unrelated to your business. As I am typing these words, someone is purchasing one of my products and money is deposited into my bank account.

Next comes your live online course, where you will teach your topic via teleseminar or webinar in four or five ninety minute sessions. When this course has been taught live even once, it can then become a home study version of the course.

This paves the way for a membership site, where your customers pay a monthly or annual fee to receive your training. Later on I'll discuss the concept of something called 'micro-continuity', where you charge a very small month fee (five or ten dollars is typical) for regular updates and content on your topic.

At some point people will begin to ask you for coaching or consulting services, and you can then decide whether this model will work for you.

And finally, hosting your own live event makes sense for your business. Start small with this and grow it over time as it feels right for you.

Just to recap, here are the pieces I am recommending for your marketing funnel:

- ✓ Free Giveaway
- ✓ Digital E-course
- ✓ Evergreen Product
- ✓ Additional Products
- ✓ Live Online Course
- ✓ Home Study Course
- ✓ Membership Site
- ✓ Mentoring/Coaching/Consulting
- ✓ Live Events

Take some time to think about what I have presented here, and write down your thoughts and ideas on how it would work for your topic. Before you say that your audience is different, or that you have some special circumstances, know that this is a proven system that has worked for hundreds of different niches and will continue to serve as a lucrative multiple streams model.

Also, think of each of your products as being a part of your 'product line'. This is a concept borrowed from the corporate world, where we as consumers think of one or two companies as being ones that will create and produce products that follow a single topic, such as cosmetics, kitchen, bathroom, and home cleaning products, and even clothing lines. This is the approach you will want to take as your business grows and matures.

Chapter 4

Being Perceived In a New Way

*Cognition refers to the way we look at things - our
perceptions, mental attitudes, and beliefs.
It includes the way we interpret things –
what we say about something
or someone or to ourself.*
~ David D. Burns

I can remember being at a large family gathering over
Thanksgiving weekend in 2010. At that time my first book
had been recently published and I was actively working on
my second and third books simultaneously. Unbeknownst to
me, the fact that I was now a published, bestselling author
was a topic of discussion among my family members. We had
a large group at the home of my Aunt and Uncle that day,
including extended family members, friends, and their
families.

A man named Mark, the husband of one of my cousins,
came up to greet me and motioned for me to follow him
through the sliding glass doors. Our large group had spilled
out onto the patio, something that is easy to do in late
November in southern California. His daughter and her
friends were there and appeared excited when they spotted
me entering the patio. They were all about nineteen or twenty

years old at that time, and usually not quite so excited to see me. I knew something was up.

Mark told this young group something in front of me that I definitely was not expecting. He said:

"Connie has written a book that will help many people. I want you to talk to her and ask her questions about what you want to do with your life. I respect what she has done and know that she can help you, too."

For the next hour I sat down with these young people and listened, truly listened to them. They shared their hopes, dreams, struggles, challenges, and goals with me in a way that I had never been privy to before, even though I had known them, at least casually for many years.

Mark had presented me as an authority, as someone who had the knowledge and the credibility to serve others and assist them as they find their way through the journey of life. Even though I was the same person they had always known, their perception of who I was had changed dramatically.

Empowering Yourself Through Publicity

I learned that day the power of having someone else vouch for your credibility, and also that it would be possible to do this for myself in the future, without the help of anyone else. This led to my study of publicity and public relations and has taken me on a journey that empowers me to present myself in exactly the way I would prefer to be perceived. Allow me to explain this point in further detail.

Many of the activities we engage in as online entrepreneurs are ones that we soon take for granted. The idea of setting up a new WordPress blog or site, posting to our blog, writing and submitting articles to the directories, building up a social media following, and creating information products are just part of doing business on the Internet.

However, all of these activities are a big deal to the people who are not a part of our world. When I first told my

Rotary Club in December of 2005 that I had started several blogs on a variety of topics they were beside themselves with excitement and wanted to know more details.

That's when I learned how to write simple press releases and distribute them online to let the world know who I was, what I was doing, and what they could expect next. You can do the same thing. Here is the exact press release I sent out at the end of December, 2014 regarding this new book you are reading:

December, 2014 Press Release

Bestselling author and online marketing strategist Connie Ragen Green announces that she is currently in the final stages of writing her eleventh book, to be titled Write. Publish. Prosper. This book will outline in great detail the process she has used over the past several years to write her previous ten books in record time, using strategies and techniques she has personally created. This innovative approach to writing is also the subject of an online course Green teaches using the exact same process.

Working online exclusively since 2006, Connie Ragen Green is a former classroom teacher and real estate broker/residential appraiser who currently resides in both the desert community of Santa Clarita, California and the beach side town of Santa Barbara, California. Having the freedom to live the life you love is her motto, and thousands of people on six continents follow her teachings to learn how to author books and build their own online empire with courses and information products.

A sought after international speaker and presenter, Connie Ragen Green also hosts her own live events and workshops twice a year. Her next event, based on this new book, is slated for the end of March, 2015 in Los Angeles, California.

'Live for a year the way others won't, then live forever the way others can't', says Green.

Connie Ragen Green has been awarded the coveted 'Better Your Best' award in 2009, hosts a podcast series named one of the 'Top 100 Small Business Podcasts' in 2014, and has had her books honored by the Small Business Book Awards three years in a row. For more information on how you can find her books and attend her live workshops, visit http://ConnieRagenGreen.com.

As you can see, I am shameless when it comes to promoting myself to the world. I also have an inner enthusiasm that I refer to as the 'Kindergarten Effect'. If you have ever spent time with a five year old, you know that they can get excited at the smallest things, such as a fly coming in through their classroom window, a neighbor wearing a bow tie for the first time, or when their parent or sibling gets a new haircut. What I am recommending here is that you approach your own business online with a similar enthusiasm, and share even your smallest accomplishments with the world through your blog posts, social media updates, and press releases.

This can all lead to you being perceived in an entirely new way than you are at this moment, and in the way you wish to be perceived. For instance, you see that I prefer to be known as a 'bestselling author and online marketing strategist', rather than by any other descriptor. This is of my choosing, and not a title or label thrust upon me by a job description or another person.

Decide how you would like to be perceived and then take the steps to make sure that's how people are introduced to you as you write your book and build your business. This will likely change over the coming years, but know that you are the one who decides how you present yourself to the world.

Now that I have introduced you to the world of online marketing and creating multiple streams of income (in

Chapter 3 and again, in more depth in *Chapter 11*), you will have a greater appreciation of what it means to be able to have input as to how others perceive you, especially when your goal is to be thought of and considered as an expert and an authority on your niche topic.

Section Three
What If You Write, Publish, And Prosper?

Chapter 5

Reaching the World with Your Message

We all have a life story and a message that can inspire others to live a better life or run a better business. Why not use that story and message to serve others and grow a real business doing it?
~ Brendon Burchard

These days it is possible to get a message half way around the world, or even further within sixty seconds or less. I've watched world events updated minute by minute on Twitter, pictorialized on Instagram, debated on Facebook, and turned into instant news feature stories on Yahoo! News. It wasn't always this way.

Long ago, back in the previous millennium, we had to wait for news to make its way to us through the traditional broadcasting and press channels of radio, television, and newspapers. Many times this news was outdated or found to be grossly incorrect by the time it reached our homes.

So please do not take this idea of being able to reach the world with your message lightly. While everything you want and need to share around your topic may not be considered newsworthy, it is important to those who are counting on you to keep them educated, informed, and inspired to change their lives for the better because of what you have to offer. No one else can deliver your message in way that will affect them in such a dramatic way. This is so important to remember at all times. In the words of John E. Lewis:

"If not us, then who?
If not now, then when?"

Try as they might, no other human being on the planet will be able to convey your message to others in the exact and specific way you have intended. Also, here is something you may not have given any thought to previously. Is it possible that you were given the challenge of working on something in your life that could be a blessing to someone else if you share with them how to improve in this area?

Journalist and anchorwoman Robin Roberts wrote about 'making your mess your message' in her book *From the Heart: Eight Rules to Live By*. This was a concept learned from her mother and one she came to live by since 2007. Robin has overcome battles with breast cancer and with myelodysplastic syndrome (MDS), a rare bone marrow disease she contracted in 2012 that resulted from her treatment for the breast cancer. Her sister turned out to be a perfect bone marrow match, and the transplant saved her life and gave her a new outlook on her life's journey. She has definitely made her mess her message and now devotes her life to helping others achieve their goals and overcome obstacles.

When I first wrote about overcoming cancer I was not prepared for the outpouring of love and support that came from people all over the world.

Writing a book and laying a foundation the way I am teaching you here is the most powerful way to get your message out to the world. Now that we can publish a blog post instantly so people can read our words and publish an audio podcast within a few short hours so others can hear our words, and take our book from conception to publication within weeks or months it is our duty and obligation to do just that.

Maya Angelou said, 'People will forget what you said. They will forget what you did. But people will never forget how you made them feel.'

I believe our goal is to leave people feeling enlightened, empowered, and enriched after reading our books. Our messages can circle the globe many times over and touch the lives of people we will never meet.

Storytelling

I believe a discussion on the topic of using storytelling in your business is in order right here. Once you think of the telling of stories as a way of reaching the world with your message you will see how everything falls into place more easily in your life and your business.

In 2004 a book was published that was entitled *Fierce Conversations: Achieving Success at Work and in Life One Conversation at a Time* by Susan Scott. Someone gave me the book as a gift and it ended up changing my life during the following year. The premise is that anyone can learn how to communicate more effectively and strengthen relationships through the art of conversation.

In this book Scott teaches her 7 Principles of Fierce Conversations, and these are:

- Master the Courage to Interrogate Reality
- Come Out from Behind Yourself into the Conversation and Make It Real
- Be Here, Prepared to Be Nowhere Else
- Tackle Your Toughest Challenge Today
- Obey Your Instincts
- Obey Your Instincts
- Let Silence Do the Heavy Lifting

I can remember reading through the book quickly and seeing this as a way to change people's perception of me at the school where I was teaching. Over the years I had come to have a reputation that I was not proud of and that was not true. I needed to get the message out about whom I really was as a person, and I used the idea of telling my story through conversations to achieve my goal.

Within about thirty days everyone at the school, from the administrators and teachers down to the parents and the custodian knew me in an entirely different way than they had before.

I can remember one of these conversations in particular, where I was speaking with (as opposed to *talking to*) another teacher about the upcoming state testing for the students. This was always a stressful time for everyone at the school and she had an idea about how we could make it easier with a different plan for how to organize and group the kids for each day's tests. She explained what she thought would work, but ended with "Too bad nobody cares what I think."

I had listened intently as she spoke, giving her my full and undivided attention. Now this was a woman who was known for running roughshod over people on a regular basis, and even though I had had numerous squabbles and several altercations with her over the years I looked her straight in the eyes after she finished speaking and said,

"I care what you think and I believe your idea is a good one. How may I support you with this?"

I thought she was going to fall over when I said that to her. She paused, took a step back, and answered,

"Let me think about it and get back to you."

I wish I could say that we became great friends after that conversation and that everything changed for me at school that day, but using storytelling and the art of conversation requires patience and strength. I will tell you that she ended up paying me a compliment at a Staff meeting several weeks later, something she had never done in the past. All of the little events add up to much bigger ones, and I was grateful to finally be on the path to better understanding.

Storytelling for business is now widely accepted and used by businesses of all sizes. It is sometimes referred to as the 'language of the senses' (LOTS) and has been explored in depth by thought leaders from all walks of life.

The concept here is a relatively simple one; when telling someone a story, share with them what you see, hear, smell, feel, and taste. By triggering this level and type of sense in someone else you bring them into the story with you. Have as your goal to activate at least two of the five senses in the people you share your next story with. I have found that the senses of smell and taste are the easiest ones, but have fun with this challenge and see how it goes for you.

You incorporate both inner dialogue and outer dialog into what you say. The inner dialogue is the internal monologue you have within your mind. It is what you are thinking or felling but not outwardly expressing. Sharing this through your story is akin to sharing a secret with the world. Your outer dialogue is what you openly share with the world.

Try this out by relating a story to someone you know. For example, I went to the grocery store early this morning and then related that story to my grandson when I returned back home. To make it more interesting I parodied the voices of the customer in line in front of me and the checker as she scanned to items on the conveyor belt. That is an example of using outer dialogue.

The main difference between just 'describing a situation' and 'telling a story' is this use of both inner and outer dialogue.

Using this style of sensory language makes an emotional connection with those listening to you. My grandson couldn't help but laugh at various points, and I could tell by his facial expressions he was enjoying the story immensely. His imagination was engaged and he was responding to my intricate details. You can bet he will remember most of my story and even share it with others in the future.

Storytelling gives us permission to explain who we are and what our vision and mission are for our life and our business. For example, I share much about my experiences of being a classroom teacher with people everywhere. I also share that I am a cancer survivor and how that impacted my decision to start an online business. You pick and choose from your own life experiences and then share the stories around them that bring everything to life. When someone reads your book or your blog they think of you as a one-dimensional being. When they hear your voice on a podcast you become two-dimensional. But reading about and listening to your stories helps flesh you out into more of a three-dimensional being. In my opinion, the only thing more riveting is meeting you in person, which most of our prospects and clients will never be able to do. Keep your stories coming, and remember to only share what you are comfortable talking about, as we are in the age of digital reality on the Internet.

Chapter 6

Living the Lifestyle You Love and Deserve

*Keep your thoughts positive, because
your thoughts become your words.
Keep your words positive, because
your words become your behavior.
Keep your behavior positive, because
your behavior becomes your habits.
Keep your habits positive, because
your habits become your values.
Keep your values positive, because
your values become your destiny.
~ Mahatma Ghandi*

My life is my own these days, and it has been since I came online to work exclusively in 2006. I am able to do what I want, when I want, and with the people I want to spend my time with in my life. Can you say the same? If not, then I will describe what my days are like and then we will delve into how you can create and live the lifestyle you love and deserve.

When I stated above that my life is my own these days I mean that I create my own schedule, choose my own tasks, and only spend time engaged in activities and with the people who enrich and uplift my daily life. This is in stark contrast to my previous life as a classroom teacher and real estate broker and appraiser, where my life was anything but my own. Most of my complaints in those days were centered around having to do things I did not enjoy or did not believe in, working with people who were far less committed to the work than I was, and having a schedule that was so inflexible as to hinder me from doing things with my family that I considered to be of great importance in my life.

In those days I needed to get up before five each morning in order to leave my home before six so that I could beat the rush hour commuters. Then I would slog my way through heavy traffic for almost an hour to make it the twenty miles to the school where I taught. All day I would teach the curriculum chosen by the school district and deliver it in the way they had prescribed. In fact, everything I said or did while I was teaching was dictated by others, and if I veered even slightly I was reprimanded publicly. Sometimes my students would lose privileges as a result of my choosing to do something that was slightly out of alignment with the district or the administrations rules. Looking back on this time in my life I sometimes wonder how I lasted for twenty years.

After school each day, which was somewhere between three-thirty and five o'clock in the afternoon I would head to my first real estate appointment. During the winter months I would finish by six, but during the summer months I had more daylight and would typically work until eight or eight-thirty each evening during the week.

During those twenty years I would leave my home when it was dark and return when it was dark, leaving me to ponder why I was working long and hard for a home I seldom saw or enjoyed during the daylight.

Weekends were not much better; I would leave by seven and return by five or six in the evening. Then I had a couple of hours of paperwork to complete before I went to bed.

Vacations were few and far between. Every other year I would leave on a Friday afternoon and return on the following Sunday, giving me eight full days to spend with family and friends before getting back to face the same schedule all over again.

I know this sounds dreary, and most of it was. The point I am emphasizing here is that I did all of this for many years out of necessity, but also as a personal choice. I truly believe we choose the life we live, and I chose the one I just described for twenty years. Whether you believe me or not, and I hope that you will take this on faith, we can step away from situations and circumstances that no longer serve us and move into ones that are loving and joyous simply by deciding to do so and then taking inspired action to move forward each day towards these goals.

In 2005 I chose an easier, more fun, and very lucrative life that I love and deserve. Looking back, I am not sure why the bright light did not come on for me much sooner, but I am grateful that it finally did and that I could turn everything around in my life. In the words of the late, great Jim Rohn:

> 'If you don't design your own life plan, chances are you'll fall into someone else's plan'.

These days I get up at various times, depending upon what I have planned for that day. It turns out I am actually a morning person, even though for the entire twenty years I was teaching and working in real estate I believed I was only a morning person because my job required me to be up and alert at an early hour of the day. The truth is that I just do not enjoy leaving my house at an early hour, unless I'm doing something fun or taking a trip to a wonderful destination.

Most days I write for an hour or so, check email, send an email message to my list, and check my statistics and other numbers for my business during the early morning; this is from approximately six-thirty or seven each morning until ten or eleven in the morning. Next comes my daily walk, which is currently for thirty minutes or so each day. I'm working on getting that back to one full hour of walking each day to improve my health and fitness level. Then I leave for the day to do some volunteer work or personal appointments before returning back home around four or five in the afternoon. I also have the time to meet with friends, family, members, or others who would like to spend some time talking with me. These meaningful conversations have changed my life over the past several years and I cannot imagine my life without these interactions.

If you have ever seen the British period drama Downton Abbey, you know that the aristocratic Crawley family is out of touch with the working class. When a cousin tries to explain that he will have time on the weekend to help with the affairs of the estate, the main character (portrayed so eloquently by Maggie Smith) exclaims, 'What is a week-end?'

I am pleased to say that now my life consists of days that are my own, no matter what the calendar says.

Your Ideal Life

Now let's discuss what you can do to live the life you love and deserve. The idea is to go from where you are today to closer to where you would like to be by taking small steps each day to make the transition into greater things for yourself.

First of all, you must believe that change of this magnitude is possible for you, and that you are exactly where you need to be right now, both physically and psychologically to ignite this type of change in your life. Once you can nod your head in agreement with this statement, you are more than half of the way there.

Now make a list of what your ideal life might look like. For some people it means flying first class to destinations of their choice on a regular basis. For others it might mean being able to enroll their children or grandchildren in private schools.

For me it has meant being able to work from my home office instead of being away from home so many hours each day. It means having homes in two cities I love and being a part of charitable organizations in both of them. It also means having both the financial freedom and the time freedom to explore new opportunities and to connect with people, causes, and organizations that resonate with me.

We cannot get what we want out of life until we know what we want. Spend some time with this, making lists of what you love and what you want to eliminate from your life right now. When I first began my journey I focused on not having to drive in rush hour traffic every day, and these days I seldom see this at all. In fact, sometimes months go by without me sitting in traffic, and it is at those times that I express my gratitude for having this new life I love and deserve.

I recommend by starting out with your daily schedule. What would an ideal day look like? Write out in detail until it makes perfect sense for you. I don't draw very well, so when I was doing this I cut out pictures and photographs from magazines and kept them in a show box. They included images of people, places, and things that I wanted to have as a part of my daily experience.

Your Life's Mission and Vision

When I first heard that all large companies, corporations, and organizations have a Mission Statement and a Vision for what they wish to achieve, I began doing this for my own life. This continues to evolve, and right now my Mission Statement states that it is my goal and intention is to reach entrepreneurs all over the world who wish to leave a job that no longer serves them and build a business they can run from home or from wherever they happen to be.

My Vision is that people must be able to earn a substantial living by working from home and serving others with their knowledge and expertise to pave the way for new entrepreneurs, and I want to be there to help them to do this easily.

How could you describe your Mission and Vision for your life and business? Who do you wish to serve? How will you enrich other people's lives?

Getting Used To Living the Life You Deserve

It is one thing to say you want to change your life completely and another to actually make it happen and sustain it for a number of years. I know because this is my reality. Sometimes I think back to the life I was living before and wonder just how I have been able to come so far in so short a time. Then I remind myself that anyone can do the same, and that it is simply a matter of making the decision and choice to change your life and then take the steps to making it happen.

Many times people will ask me how I became so successful so quickly and I will joke that I am an overnight success that took years to manifest. The truth is that change occurs at the cellular level and that every action you take is either moving you closer to or further away from your goals. That is why it is so important to plan out exactly what you want to achieve and to write it down as a reminder of where you are now and where you are going each day.

For example, a book doesn't get written overnight. In the next section I'll go into great detail as to how you get started with an idea and then do the research and create an outline before you begin to write. Then you schedule a time to write each day and over a period of weeks your book begins to take shape and resemble what you originally had planned to write. As soon as my outline is complete I like to write five hundred to a thousand words each day until I get to ten thousand words. Then I step back for a few days and do not give the book any thought until I am ready to write again. By that point I am pretty much filling in the blanks for each section of each chapter, and it is truly a joy to continue writing.

Section Four
What Is The Step By Step Process?

Chapter 7

Pre-Writing, Research, And Planning

*Productivity is never an accident. It is always
the result of a commitment to excellence,
intelligent planning, and focused effort.*
~ Paul J. Meyer

Your goal is to be as productive as possible each and every day, and knowing how to make the most of pre-writing, research, and planning is the way to do that for your online business endeavors.

Pre-writing is the process of getting at least some of your ideas out on paper, or into a word processing document before you officially begin. This has been particularly worthwhile for me as someone who is still relatively new to the world of writing and publishing on a regular basis.

Your ideas may be ones you have had bottled up inside of you for months or years, could come out of a conversation you have with someone about your topic, or might be based on books you have read or other media you have been exposed to. Whatever the case may be, take the time to get it all out before you even begin to organize this content into a logical form.

Typically I begin a new document in Word when I decide to write a new book, where I add everything I think might be included in the final manuscript. This is done without editing or researching or even questioning whether it truly belongs. Sometimes I come across a quote or a story about something that seems like it could be connected and I don't want to lose it by censoring my thoughts and ideas during this preliminary stage. Or I have a conversation with someone and some of the ideas we discuss strike a chord with me that may have merit in what I will be writing.

When I am away from my computer I will write things down in my notebook, and as soon as I am back at home I transfer these notes to this document and save it. It is said that the dullest ink is better than the sharpest memory when it comes to remembering what you want to write.

Research

The research you will do for your book is crucial to its success. I would encourage you to take your time with this portion of the process and to embrace it joyfully. Those who cut corners in this area, out of boredom or the perceived need to save time, are shortchanging themselves and their future by doing so. Remember that you are building something that will give you the credibility as an authority on your topic. All experts and authorities take the time and make the effort to do valuable research before they begin any project. This begins by looking at other people's work on your niche topic, and Amazon is the perfect place to do this.

Name three books that have been written on your topic. Have you read them? Are you familiar with the authors? Look through these books, physically or digitally to see if you can get some ideas for your own book. Especially look through the Table of Contents to see which aspects of your topic they thought to be most important.

Also, if you find that you have not read books on your topic by authors who are known in your niche, this is the perfect time to remedy that situation. We must stay abreast of what is happening in our field and who the 'movers and shakers' are. Authors would definitely fall into this category as 'key players' to know and learn from as your business grows.

One of my clients is an expert in the area of accountability, and I offered to do some research for her before she began writing her own book. I was surprised to see as many books around this topic as I did, and wanted to see which keywords they were focusing on. Here are four of them that I found to be most relevant to what she would be writing about.

1. *Accountability: The Key to Driving a High-Performance Culture* by Greg Bustin
   Keyword phrases - purpose, urgency, team work, leadership
2. *Crucial Accountability: Tools for Resolving Violated Expectations, Broken Commitments, and Bad Behavior*, Second Edition by Kerry Patterson, et al.
   Keyword phrases - positive deviance, disappointments, expectations
3. *Winning with Accountability: The Secret Language of High-Performing Organizations* by Henry J. Evans
   Keyword phrases - language of accountability, ownership, creating a high-accountability culture
4. *QBQ! The Question Behind the Question: Practicing Personal Accountability at Work and in Life* by John G. Miller
   Keyword phrases - personal accountability, procrastination, integrity, communication

You can see that for each book I looked at I chose the keyword phrases that the author used in their main sections, chapter titles, and sub-titles. Many of these were familiar to me, while others, such as 'high accountability culture' were new to my thinking on this topic.

The idea with this research is to never copy what another person has done, but instead to learn from them and to give them credit if you make a reference in your own book to something they have mentioned, even in a small way. That is the beginning of a concept known as coopetition, where people in the same niche cooperatively compete in a way that helps both to be elevated in the eyes of readers everywhere.

As your research continues, make a notes of which books and authors you are already familiar with on your topic. Make a mental note to further connect with these authors in the near future. Leave a review on Amazon for the books you have already read, and plan to do so for those you will read later on. This is a marketing strategy that will help you to be seen as an authority on your topic by others who are involved in your niche.

Keywords

It's important to take a half a step back right now and have a more complete discussion about keywords. Your keywords are the words and phrases others use when they are looking for more information on your topic. We all use these when we go to Google to look up information.

For example, if I am thinking about buying a new home I may type in the words 'real estate' and see what comes up. I will quickly see that using this phrase is much too general to give me the results I am looking for.

Keywords are considered to be 'main' or 'primary', 'mid-tale', or 'long tail' in nature. 'Real estate' is definitely a primary or main keyword phrase that would return very general results.

My next attempt might be to type in 'homes in south Florida' and this would be somewhat better, but still not exactly what I want or need. This is an example of a 'mid-tale' keyword.

Now I could type in 'three bedroom homes for sale in North Miami Beach' but this could be too specific. This is an example of a 'long tail' keyword. However, if I were the homeowner or the real estate agent trying to sell a three bedroom home in North Miami Beach this could be perfect.

Over time you will make a list of your primary, mid-tail, and long tail keywords for your niche topic and use them for the titles of your blog posts, podcasts, and other marketing materials. In the beginning I would print out a list of these and keep them pinned to the book shelf next to my desk, but over time you get to know your keywords so well they will stick in your brain and be available whenever and wherever you want to recall them to grow your business.

However, you may still want to do this periodically to see if there is anything new or keywords you may have long forgotten to use in your business.

Planning

The planning stage is where you begin to organize all of your thoughts, ideas, and knowledge into an outline. I would recommend that you do this in a general 'big picture' way at first and then narrow it down into the sections and chapters that will comprise your book.

Think of this as moving from your old residence into a new home. You have lots of furniture, boxes, and miscellaneous items that need to physically move from one location to another, but you don't want it just dumped into the driveway or front yard or living room. Instead, you want everything to be moved carefully into the room in the new house where it belongs.

Your book is the same way. For example, I would not write about the process of designing a cover for your book at this point in our study of this topic. It would feel out of place for you as the reader because there is so much more to cover before we come to that discussion.

Everyone works differently when it comes to planning a book and then creating an outline that can be used to write more quickly and efficiently. I tend to be more linear, but you may enjoy the process more fully by creating a mind map. The best way to plan out your book is the way that works for you and will make your writing come more quickly and easily.

In my linear planning I tend to start with the four questions I use for every book I write, presentation I give, and course I teach. Here they are:

1. WHY is (YOUR TOPIC) so important for your target audience to learn more about?
2. WHAT is (YOUR TOPIC) by definition?
3. WHAT IF your community utilized the strategies you are teaching us about (YOUR TOPIC), what would their life be like in thirty days, ninety days, one year?
4. HOW does (YOURTOPIC) work in a step-by-step process?

I'd like to give you some history on where these four questions originated and how I came to feature them so prominently in my books, presentations, and online courses.

I first heard about the four questions from Alex Mandossian as a part of a course he was teaching back in 2007. When he suggested I use them for a project I was working on I made the decision to give it a try. After adjusting the questions to better suit my purpose I soon realized this was an excellent way to frame every project I would take on in the future. Alex credits this concept to David Kolb, the author of *Experiential Learning: Experience as the Source of*

Learning and Development. The quote he uses to describe what he is teaching with experiential learning is 'Tell me, and I will forget. Show me, and I may remember. Involve me, and I will understand." ~Confucius 450 BC.

Since that time I was introduced to a book by Simon Sinek, *Start with Why: How Great Leaders Inspire Everyone to Take Action* by my colleague Miguel de Jesus. Sinek's quote is 'People don't buy what you do; they buy why you do it. And what you do simply proves what you believe.'

These were deep, thought provoking ideas when I was first exposed to them, but now that they have had some time to simmer I feel like I better understand what they mean and how I can apply these ideas to my own life and business.

Start by writing or typing out the four questions. Decide how you can change them to better suit your topic. Then decide where each part of the information you want to share in your book would fit.

Remember the concept of placing items into your new home. Use this as you decide which section your knowledge will fit into most effectively.

This is the example I came up with for one of my clients who works in the area of getting organized and decluttering for entrepreneurs:

Section I – *Why* Do We Care About Getting Organized?
Section II – *What Is* Organization For Entrepreneurs?
Section III – *What If* We Eliminate Clutter?
Section IV – *How Do We* Get Organized And Declutter?

You can see that I adjusted these four questions in a way that makes sense for her topic. Do this for your own topic and see what ideas you come up with. Next to each one, write a few lines or a paragraph detailing what you intend on including in your book about each of them. Also, start a list of the topics, ideas, and information you would wish to include in your writing.

I like to write down everything I may include in my book, along with the details of where I can find more information and even what I was thinking when I decided to include additional information. All of this may not make it into my outline, but it makes the process flow well and gets me closer to the point of being able to write my book by simply filling in the blanks. We'll discuss this further in the next chapter.

Chapter 8

Creating Your Outline

Organizing ahead of time makes the work more enjoyable.
Even chefs cut up the onions and
have the ingredients lined up ahead of
time and have them ready to go.
When everything is organized it makes
everything so much easier and fun.
~ Anne Burrell

Your detailed outlined is the backbone of your book. Based upon the planning sessions you spent time with during the previous chapter (*Chapter 7* – Pre-Writing, Research, and Planning), create an outline loosely based on what you have already written down. Your goal is to finally have in front of you a detailed and precise outline from which your book will be written in a way where the words flow and the book takes shape effortlessly. Think of this as a blueprint, as if you are about to break ground on the world's next skyscraper or residence. What you put into this part of the process will pay off in spades as you write. My own experience has shown me that the proper outline will allow you to practically channel the book you are supposed to write, in an amazingly short period of time.

While you are creating your outline, also start a document where you will take your notes. This is where I like to write down my ideas, favorite quotes, links to references I am using, and anything else that will be related to my book but not actually included in what I publish. I referred to this document in the beginning of the previous chapter. Later on it's interesting to go back to this document and recall what you were thinking during this period of time. This document is more than a journal or notepad, and is an integral part of your writing process.

First I come up with a Thesis Statement, which I define as the Big Idea upon which my book will be based. For example, my Thesis Statement for this book is 'I believe that anyone can write a full length book within the next four to six weeks, build a platform around this book to be seen as an authority in a specific niche, and set up a marketing funnel that will lead to a lucrative online business'. Everything I include in my outline will support this Thesis Statement.

The Four Questions (also introduced previously in *Chapter 7*) come next. I find that if I use the Four Questions, thinking of each of them as a separate section of my book, everything comes together much more quickly than if I would attempt to organize it any other way.

At this point I also suggest creating at least a *working* title for your book. It can always be changed at any time prior to the book's publication, but for now you will want to refer to it by name, instead of just thinking of your writing in vague and abstract terms.

You may remember from high school the outlines that were required by your English teacher and perhaps from other instructors as well. Those had a very rigid and specific format that you do not need to follow here. I can remember having a history teacher one year who flipped out because I had not adhered to the guidelines and used lower case letters instead of numbers in one section of my outline. Now that you are an entrepreneur you make the rules as to how to accomplish your goals, so I will share with you what continues to work for me in regards to outlining a book.

We will return to the example from my client who is an expert in the area of getting organized and eliminating clutter. These were the Four Questions we came up with for her book's outline:

Section I – *Why* Do We Care About Getting Organized?
Section II – *What Is* Organization For Entrepreneurs?
Section III – *What If* We Eliminate Clutter?
Section IV – *How Do We* Get Organized And Declutter?

The next step is to brainstorm some logical topics that could be turned into chapters for the book. Based on what we have already, these are the possible chapter titles we came up with:

- ✓ Growing up with clutter

- ✓ Everyone has clutter

- ✓ Is it normal not to have any 'stuff'

- ✓ Psychological reasons for having clutter

- ✓ Recycling paper and other clutter

- ✓ Getting organized as an entrepreneur

- ✓ Organizing your home office space

- ✓ Feeling good about your living and work space

- ✓ Making a Plan

- ✓ 30 Day decluttering plan

- ✓ Spot organizing

- ✓ Staying on top of clutter forever

Now you will want to organize and reorder these chapter titles in a way that will make sense from beginning to end. The mind works in a linear fashion to make sense of the data it has to deal with, so this step is crucial to the outlining process at this point in your writing.

Next, choose two or three chapter titles to fit into each of your four Sections.

Section I – Why do we care about getting organized?
   Chapter 1 – Growing up with clutter
   Chapter 2 – Everyone has clutter
Section II – What Is Organization For An Entrepreneur?
   Chapter 3 – Is it normal not to have any stuff?
   Chapter 4 – Getting organized as an entrepreneur
Section III – What If We Eliminate Clutter?
   Chapter 5 – Psychological reasons for having clutter
   Chapter 6 – Feeling good about a living/work space
   Chapter 7 – Spot organizing
Section IV – How Do We Get Organized And Declutter?
   Chapter 8 – Organizing Your Home office space
   Chapter 9 – Recycling paper and other clutter
   Chapter 10 – Making a plan
Section V – Success at Last!
   Chapter 11 – 30 Day decluttering plan
   Chapter 12 – Staying on top of clutter forever

But wait, what have we here? There is now a fifth Section entitled 'Success at Last!' Is that permitted?

Yes, of course. You are the author and an authority on your topic. The outline must fit into what you have in your mind as your end goal, and not the other way around.

The final step for this part of the process is to go one level deeper with your outline. For each chapter, write at least three sentences that can be starting points for your writing. These will become your book's Sub-Sections and are the key to simplifying the process of writing a book quickly and easily.

If you are interested in a word count for your book at this point, think of each chapter as consisting of about fifteen hundred words. So in this example with twelve chapters you would have about eighteen thousand words.

There are also more parts to your book, such as the Dedication, the Foreword, the Preface, the Introduction, the Conclusion, the Resources section, and additional content, such as Addendums and other end matter, so your book will end up with approximately twenty-five thousand words by the time it goes to print.

Don't be so concerned with this number, and certainly do not allow it to overwhelm you, as I will be explaining in great detail how each piece of this process of writing a book will come together seamlessly over the next four to six weeks.

A completed outline allows you to simply 'fill in the blanks' of each section after you get moving and find your own writing and creative rhythm around your book. Then set a goal for yourself to write one or two five hundred word sections each day, or whatever works for you. Even though this book supports the premise of writing a full length book in four to six weeks, you must march to the beat of your own drummer. I have written and published a book in seven days, written several within four to six weeks, and take four months to complete another. The only constant in this process is that the outline makes it all come together in a seamless way.

Chapter 9

Advanced Writing and Creation Strategies

First, make yourself a reputation for being a creative genius. Second, surround yourself with partners who are better than you are. Third, leave them to go get on with it.
~ David Ogilvy

If you pull several books randomly from your book shelf and go through the Table of Contents of each one of them you will see that each one is put together differently. What this tells us is that there is no right or wrong way to build the inner parts of your book, but there are some standard components I want you to be aware of as you are writing. It's best to know what the possibilities are and then choose what works best for you than to not be aware of what has been done by others and to just move forward blindly.

I will simply list the possible components here and then go into great detail about each one further in this chapter. Here they are:

- ✓ Front Matter (includes your Dedication, Foreword, Preface, Acknowledgements, and Introduction)
- ✓ Dedication
- ✓ Table of Contents
- ✓ Foreword

- ✓ Preface
- ✓ Acknowledgements
- ✓ Introduction
- ✓ Sections/Chapters
- ✓ End Matter

The 'End Matter' may be referred to as any of these:

- ✓ Epilogue
- ✓ Afterword
- ✓ Conclusion
- ✓ Postscript
- ✓ Backword (my own invention!)
- ✓ Appendix(es)or Addendum

Your Dedication Page

Let's start with a discussion of the Dedication page of your book. Most likely you have read dedications in hundreds of books over the years. But have you ever taken the time to deconstruct what the author wrote and categorize it as a style of dedication? Probably not.

How will you choose the person or people to dedicate your book to in the first place? You already know who the important people in your life are. There may be family members that had a major impact on your life, either when you were a child or much more recently. You also have someone who was instrumental in helping you get your book off the ground, through emotional support, financial support, or actual physical help in putting your book together.

If this is the first book you will have written and published, you may want to dedicate it to someone in your immediate family. But also think about an important business partner or colleague, a college professor, book editor, research assistant, sibling, or even a close friend. This is a very personal choice, so there really is no wrong decision.

If there is a second person that is just as important to you and the writing of your book, don't be afraid to dedicate your book to both of them. But limit it to no more than a couple of names, or you will greatly diminish the importance of your dedication. You still can list all the other important people who you want to give recognition to, in the acknowledgement's section of your book. This retains the dedication as a very high honor.

The dedication page is your opportunity to explain why you chose the person you did for this great honor. This also serves as an explanation to the dedicatee, as well as to your readers. This type of an explanation in your dedications helps to create an emotional connection with your reader, an opportunity you do not want to miss. Everyone reads the dedication page. Making this emotional connection with readers at this early stage is critical to the success of your book in the long run. In order to get book buyers to buy your book in the first place, and to then get them to read the entire book, like what they read, leave you a positive review, and then want to purchase more of your books in the future, it is imperative to make this emotional connection with them.

Over these past four years with my plethora of books I have dedicated them to friends and family members, both living and dead, to special neighbors and service providers, as well as to my Rotary Club and its members.

From my experience I have found that dedications fall into two categories; they are either formal or informal. Within those two distinctions there are many more options, so suffice it to say that you can do whatever you like. Here are some examples of what may work for your book.

Let's begin with examples of Informal dedications:

Informal and Simple: 'This is for you, Mom.'
Informal and Complex: ' This is for you, Mom. Thanks for always being there for me. And thank you for always making my favorite lasagna when I was feeling down.'

With an Anecdote: ' To Tory, for those years of going to the beach, and walking all the way there and back. I will never forget you!'

Informal and In Memory Of: 'In memory of Kim Story. You touched our lives with grace and humility. You will never be forgotten.'

Next comes the Formal dedications:

Formal and Simple: 'For my Mother.'

Formal and Complex: ' I dedicate this to my Mother; you were my first role model.'

Formal, With an Anecdote: 'This book is dedicated to Theresa Root, for her kindness, love, and devotion, and for her endless support when Mother was ill; her spirit of selflessness will always be remembered.'

Formal and In Memory Of: 'For David Asher, in memoriam. You walked the earth for such a short time, yet left your imprint on us forever.'

In my own books I have used various combinations and takes on these themes, and the people I have dedicated my books to always feel that I have singled them out as special people in my life experience. That has always been my intention, and you will choose the people and words that make the most sense to you as well.

Next comes the Table of Contents. This is usually inserted after your writing of the book is completed, but this is where it will be physically located within your book when it is finally put together.

The Foreword

The Foreword, most commonly misspelled as Forward, is the place for a guest author of your choosing to explain to the reader why they should be reading your book. The Foreword of a book is also a major selling tool for the book, if it is written properly, and by the appropriate person, You, as the book's author will gain much credibility in the eyes of your readers if this part of your book is written well and by the appropriate person. Remember that you should not write the Foreword yourself. Instead, you can use the Preface as well as the Introduction to say what needs to be said about the book from your perspective.

So if you are not going to be the one to write the Foreword, then who should you choose and what direction will you give them? Let's discuss that here.

As for whom you will ask to write this important section of your book for you, think about the people who have supported you in your life during the past five years or so. I do not feel like it is appropriate to have this come from a close friend or family member, unless they are known in your field or somehow have an occupation or a business where they are recognized in their own right. For example, we have a judge in our family, and he may be the perfect person to write a Foreword for a family member.

You will want to give this guest author some direction as to what type of information you want them to include. Make sure to give them a copy of your manuscript. Even if you are not yet finished, send them a document with as much as you have so they will have the opportunity to read it and know what it is about. Make sure to let them know who your target audience is so they will know the type of people they are writing to with their Foreword.

I like to ask them to write somewhere between seven hundred and fifty and fifteen hundred words. Then explain that you need for them to add to your credibility on your topic with what they write for you. This begins with them writing about how and when they first came to know you.

Remember that I mentioned earlier how you are trying to make an emotional connection with the reader, so you want the reader to like you and your story. The person writing your foreword is entrusted to the job of helping to get the reader to believe and trust what they have to say about you as the book's author and the book itself. Tell them to keep the tone simple, straightforward, and personal, but to keep the writing tight. They may want to include short anecdotes and real world examples that illustrate the theme of the book. Anecdotes are an important way to help the reader like you and your story. Finally, ask them to share why you are a credible person to have written this book.

This may seem like a very tall order for you to give someone, but I have found that people are honored that you have asked them and will rise to the occasion.

The Preface

The Preface is a place for you as the author to tell the reader how this book came into being, and why it was written in the first place. It should build credibility for both the author and the book. The Preface is very similar to the Foreword, except that the Preface is written by you. The Preface is also an important selling tool for the book. Here the author should explain why they wrote the book, and how they came to write it. The author should be showing the reader why they are worth reading.

Remember what I said earlier about making an emotional connection with your readers. The Preface is yet another opportunity to do so. Show your passion around your subject matter and the inspiration for wanting to write the book.

The Acknowledgements Page

The Acknowledgments is where you recognize and thank the people who have been helpful in your process of writing your book, either directly or indirectly. This could include your family members, editor, illustrator, graphic designer, Mentor, cover designer, and publisher. Instead of simply acknowledging them, briefly explain the reason(s) why you have mentioned them.

Be sure to plan out your Acknowledgements page with some serious thought while you are developing, writing, and finishing your book. Also, look through books on your bookshelf to find ones you can emulate. Remember that you want to make that emotional connection with your reader, so try to find one or two from authors you have read who have achieved this goal. If reading their acknowledgements make you want to get to know them better, they have hit the mark with this.

Make sure that you are honest and sincere with what you say about others here, and not at all flippant or cavalier with your remarks. Inside jokes have no place here, and you want the reader to see that you have surrounded yourself with smart, interesting, and productive people. This is an excellent reflection on you and makes your book worth reading.

The Introduction

The Introduction introduces the material that is covered in the book. Here is the place where you can set the stage for the reader, and prepare them for what can be expected from reading the entire book. The Introduction is a way for the author to grab the reader, and intensify their desire to find out more as they gobble up your content. In the Introduction you tell the reader what is to be revealed in much greater detail if they continue reading. Let's break this down even more so that your Introduction will be an excellent one.

You want to emphasize and explain how your book is going to help them to achieve their goals. This explanation enables you to turn this section of your book into a powerful sales tool for you to use to hook the reader right away so they will not only buy, but also read what you have written.

Those who buy your book don't truly care why you wrote it; they simply want to know how your information will help them. This makes sense if you think about it because it is just human nature for us to care about ourselves in this way. Your Introduction gives you an excellent opportunity to convince the buyer that your book is the very best one available on your topic that can help them immediately and completely.

You do this by grabbing the reader's attention. Make a shocking claim (but one you can back up), use a quote from someone famous, or share some dramatic facts or a news headline. What are the concerns or challenges of your target audience that your book will help to solve? Make an effort to put yourself into their shoes, and explain why they should buy your book today.

For example, in my Introduction for this book I make a dramatic claim regarding being able to write and publish a book in the next four to six weeks. I back this up by stating that I have done this with great success on numerous occasions over the past four years. Also, I share that at least eighty percent of the population would like to write a book, yet fewer than ten percent ever do so.

You must attempt to understand some of the challenges and problems of your audience that led them to seek out books on your topic. What keeps them awake at night? Why are they unable to solve these problems and challenges on their own? Explain to your audience why and how you know about these problems and challenges and why you are the person with the answers and solutions. Convince them that you want to share this information with them and will do so within the pages of your book.

Features and benefits are used to make sales of everything you can imagine, and books are no exception. Features explain what something *is*, and benefits describe what something *does*. Let's focus on benefits here, as they are what will sell your book. Include several of your most important benefits as you write the Introduction. These should be both general and specific, where you discuss both the overall benefits to anyone reading as well as more personal benefits for someone who is your ideal prospect.

This is also the section where you give the reader an idea about how your book is organized and arranged. Your books Table of Contents has already given them an overview, but this is the time and place to share some other insights regarding where they will find what they need that are not reflected in the table of contents.

There is also a section called the Prologue, which is used in novels and literary works. The Prologue is an opening to a story that establishes the setting and gives background details, often some earlier story that ties into the main one, and other miscellaneous information. It may be used to give more detailed background information that is pertinent to the story, describe a scene that took place in the past, or to tell the story from a different perspective and point of view, or even a different point in time.

We do not use a Prologue in a non-fiction book, but I wanted to include it here as a point of reference.

Sections, Chapters, and Sub-Sections

This is the meat of your book. Earlier (in the sub-section on Planning in *Chapter 7*) I explained how I use a form of the 4 Questions to create my own Sections in my books. This is so effective I also do it with the online courses I create and in my live workshops and presentations.

You may want to review *Chapter 8* on Creating Your Outline before moving forward with what I am sharing here.

Within each of my Sections I then decide which of my chapter titles will make the cut and will actually be included as Chapters within each Section. There is no rule for this, but I prefer to have at least two Chapters in each of my Sections. This is where I rewrite some of the chapter titles to sound more like what I will include.

Write. Publish. Prosper.

For each Chapter I now write one sentence on three different topics that will become my Chapter's Sub-Sections. Sometimes it seems difficult to come up with three different sub-topics for each Chapter, but please trust me on this. Breaking it down into this final step will make your writing flow so much more easily when you begin putting your book together.

End Matter

The final Section(s) of your book are referred to as the End Matter and there are different names for these. They include:

- ✓ Epilogue
- ✓ Afterword
- ✓ Conclusion
- ✓ Summary
- ✓ Postscript
- ✓ Backward (my own invention!)
- ✓ Appendix(es)or Addendum
- ✓ Resources

I tend to choose two or three of these for my books these days. For example, in this book I chose to have a Conclusion, two Appendices (A and B) and then the Resources section at the very end. It's entirely up to you, so choose something for now just to add to your outline and know that you may change these at any time before your book is published.

Sometimes there is confusion as to what should be included as an Addendum and what would make up an Appendix. Let's clear that up right now.

Addendum or Appendix

The Appendix and an Addendum are similar in that both can be short sections making up the end matter of a book. However, they each contain different kinds of information, and are included for different reasons.

An Appendix is a section of extra information that is useful to the reader. For example, in this book I included white papers written by two colleagues on their respective writing processes, as well as an example of a 7 Day E-Course and a Special Report. For simplicity and clarity I chose to separate these into two Appendices, Appendix A and Appendix B.

The plural form for appendix can be either Appendices (the more traditional) or Appendixes (more recently accepted and not yet comfortable to me).

On the other hand, an Addendum is a section consisting of new material that is added after the first edition or first printing of a book. The author may be needing to correct something from the original book, updating the information in the book, or simply providing an explanation for the author's work. In any case, it is an afterthought.

The plural of Addendum can be either the more traditional Addenda or Addendums (more recently accepted).

Quotations

I love to hand pick quotations to include at the beginning of my Sections and/or my Chapters.

There are a variety of sources for these
http://www.BrainyQuote.com/
http://www.QuoteGarden.com/
http://www.WisdomQuotes.com/

The Order of Things

So now let's review the order of things that will be included in your outline and thus, in your final manuscript for your book. They would be:

- ✓ Dedication
- ✓ Table of Contents
- ✓ Foreword
- ✓ Preface
- ✓ Acknowledgements
- ✓ Introduction
- ✓ Sections/Chapters/Sub-Sections
- ✓ End Matter (Conclusion, Appendix, Resources, Addendum, etc.)

You can now see that it is imperative to understand the basic differences in these book sections in order to produce a professional looking and complete book. Each section is clearly different, and each performs a specific function in a book. Therefore, an author will need to put a lot of thought and effort into producing these vital sections. As I've stated earlier, this is all by personal choice; there are no hard and fast rules that say you must include anything I'm teaching here, and even in my previous books I have deviated from this. You will know what is right for you and your topic.

Getting Your Book Published

Now it's time for you to decide which publication process will be best for you and your book. Because there are so many possibilities for this, let's take time to review the recent history of book publishing.

Before the turn of the century, and by this I am referring to the last millennium, it was necessary to work with an agent and a traditional publisher in order to get your book in print.

You are more than likely familiar with some of these large publishing houses, with names like Random House, Simon and Schuster, Harper Collins, Penguin Group, and a few others.

Additionally, each of these publishers has many subsidiaries under them, such as Bantam Books and Dell Publishing being under the Random House name. This can all become quite complicated, but the idea is that each publishing company would then be able to specialize in a variety of genres of writing, thus serving the reading public more completely.

The problem with this structure is that authors like you and I get shut out many times when we seek representation for our writing and want to have it published. Add to this the facts that each publisher can only publish a limited number of books each year and that they keep the lion's share of the proceeds of the sales of the books they represent, and often times there is very little left over for the author.

Digital rights become an even bigger issue, with the author losing control over what they can do with their own content.

'Vanity' publishing, meaning that the author paid for their book to be in print, came about as early as the nineteenth and early twentieth century's. At this time it was common for authors to pay the costs of publishing their books if they were able to afford it. The benefits to these authors included more control of their work and greater profits.

Authors who published in this way included Lewis Carroll (Alice's Adventures in Wonderland), Rudyard Kipling, Mark Twain, E. Lynn Harris, Zane Grey, Upton Sinclair, Carl Sandburg, Edgar Rice Burroughs, George Bernard Shaw, Edgar Allan Poe, Henry David Thoreau, Walt Whitman and Anaïs Nin also self-published some or all of their works. This was not a perfect model early on, and one example of this is Mark Twain's publishing business, that ended up in bankruptcy.

Interestingly, the 1939 novel Gadsby, written as a lipogram, was published through a vanity press when the author, Ernest Vincent Wright was unable to find a traditional publisher for his unusual work. A lipogram is a style of constrained writing consisting in writing paragraphs or longer works in which a particular letter or group of letters is avoided—usually a common vowel, and frequently 'E', which is the most common letter in the English language. Gadsby's more than fifty thousand words were written without including the letter 'E' anywhere within its pages.

Everything began to change in 1989, when software engineer Tim Berners-Lee invented the World Wide Web. He and his team outlined a plan that would make the Internet accessible to the general population. In 1993, it was announced that this technology will be free for anyone to use. Modern self-publishing was born when this seed was planted in the minds of authors around the world.

I've included references to how all of this came about in the Resources section at the end of the book, and if you are interested in this part of our history then I would encourage you to go through the materials I have provided. Knowing that you can now exercise full and complete control over everything you write is a fantastic feeling.

Self Publishing for the Twenty First Century

These days it is easier than ever to publish your own books, and we have Amazon to thank in a major way for getting the ball rolling. In 2005, Amazon acquired BookSurge and CustomFlix (they changed the name to Create Space in 2007). In October of 2009, the Create Space and Book Surge brands were merged under the Create Space name to become the publishing leader for independent content creators and publishers. When I found out about this in late fall of 2009 I knew that the world had changed in favor of authors who wanted to get their messages out to the world via a published book that could easily get into the hands of readers all over the planet. As a direct result, my first book was published through Create Space in July of 2010.

Kindle or Paperback

Although I have experimented with different methods and strategies, I find that first publishing my books in paperback and then releasing the Kindle version about six months later is best. By not making the print and digital versions available simultaneously, I am making more sales and also having twice the opportunity to market my title to the world.

You will have to decide which strategy is best for your target audience and topic. The choices would be to release your book as a paperback version first and then delay the release of it on Kindle; to do this in reverse; or to release both versions simultaneously. I came to the strategy I am using after trial and error with my first five books.

Cover Design

It turns out that people do judge a book by its cover, so make the effort to have an appealing on for your book. I get ideas from other people's books, and these days we can do that by searching on Amazon or visiting our local book stores. You may want to look through my books to see what you like and what you don't like about the covers I have used. My page on Amazon is at ConnieRagenGreenBooks.com.

Finding a cover designer is not as difficult as you may think. Ask for recommendations from authors you know in person or through social media. There may be someone locally that you can connect with, or you may find that working with someone virtually, as I have always done, is the fastest and easiest way to get what you want done.

Write. Publish. Prosper.

One last comment about cover designs; colors appear differently on different computers and in the physical world. Get used to referring to the colors you want for your design by using their hexadecimal equivalent. All colors may be specified as an RGB triplet or in hexadecimal format (also referred to as a hex triplet). In the Resources section at the end of this book I have provided two references for you to choose colors easily in this way.

Chapter 10

Getting Your Book Written

The writing process for me is pretty much always
the same - it's a solitary experience.
~ Sheryl Crow

Now that you have decided how to publish your book it's time to get back to the actual writing and completion of your book.

Getting into the habit of daily writing is easier for some than it is for others, so you will have to gage your progress based on where you are at this moment in time.

I have shared with you earlier in this book that I was a writer who did not write, and those years will filled with the frustration of knowing that I could achieve something that would be meaningful in my life if I would just be able to sit down and write on a regular basis. I believe that anyone can get into the habit of writing if you approach it with the right perspective.

This includes knowing when your 'prime time' hours are each day, scheduling a time to write each day, and having an outline to work from so that you are finally just filling in the blanks to get your book written as quickly as possible. Let's explore each of these in greater detail.

Prime Time

You may be familiar with the concept of prime time as it relates to the world of television. It is the block of broadcast programming taking place during the middle of the evening for television programming; more specifically, it refers to the time between eight o'clock and eleven in the evening, when the television stations have the greatest number of viewers and the highest potential for advertising revenues.

You have your own 'prime time' each day as well, and I define this as the block of hours when you are the most alert and enthusiastic and have the highest potential for creativity and productivity. These will be different for each person, but you more than likely already have a good idea of when these hours occur for you each day.

My prime time is from about six-thirty to eleven each morning. As I am typing this it is nine-forty in the morning for me, and I am still in the mode and frame of mind of being able to write, think clearly, and draw upon my memory for the specific stories and references I want to include in this book. Within an hour or so these feelings will begin to fade and I will once again sink into my daily routine. I may have moments throughout the day where sparks of creativity and higher level thought occur, but for the most part my writing and creative thinking is over until early tomorrow morning. I insist upon having quiet time to work during these precious hours at least four days a week, and that may expand to six days a week if I am writing a book or creating a course I will teach online.

I recommend that you take a few minutes right now to discover when you own prime time occurs each day and to then make the necessary adjustments to use that time to write and to create.

Scheduling a Time to Write

Writing each day needs to be important to you if it is to get done. Make it an appointment in your book and you will begin to take it more seriously in your life. My standing appointment to write begins by seven each morning. I prefer to do this a minimum of three days a week, and it may increase to six or even seven days a week when I am finishing a book. The sense of accomplishment you will feel after you have completed your appointment will lift you higher and hasten your success.

Knowing your 'Prime Time' is crucial here, as you will want to write when your mind and body are the most alert and creative.

Writer's Block

Even the most prolific writers experience something referred to as 'writer's block' once in awhile. This can best be described as a time when you sit down in front of your computer screen and just can't think of anything to write about.

The outlining process I am teaching here can help prevent this most of the time, but you still must be prepared for those times when the words do not come to you so easily.

When this happens to me, and it still occurs once in a great while, I just start writing about an experience that has just happened to me. Today that could be my recent trip to Europe, getting ready for the holidays, or spending time with friends I rarely see any longer. By taking this time for free writing I have opened up my mind and senses to the world around me, giving me the chance to share my experiences in a way that I might soon forget otherwise. Sometimes I turn these into blog posts or posts on social media, but the end result is always the same; my longing to get back to the task of writing my book.

By visualizing what it will be like to have this eleventh book completed, my mind is anxious to stop the free flow of writing and get back to the outline I have carefully created to keep my thoughts and ideas organized in the manner in which I wish to present them to the world. I think of all of the readers who will be impacted by my knowledge and the experiences I'm sharing and that gets me back on track quite readily.

Back to Your Outline

Once I discovered the power of having an outline to work from while writing a book, it was possible for me to complete my work much more efficiently, and you'll be able to do this as well.

Return now to the outline you began creating back in *Chapter 6*. This is the time to fill it in completely, as a partially completed outline will do more to impede your progress than anything else.

Make sure you have four or more Sections, at least two Chapters within each Section, and three (or more) Sub-Sections within each Chapter.

Writing

There is no substitute for actually sitting down and writing, but this all becomes simple when you are working off of your completed outline. It is like 'filling in the blanks' as your ideas flow. I've attempted to write books with and without an outline, and the outline method wins, hands down.

Choose the date you want to finish your book, and then plan in reverse how much time you'll need to spend in getting it written.

Some authors love the actual writing process, while others enjoy the idea of 'having written'. Either way, you must make this a priority in your life if you are to be successful as an author, publisher, and entrepreneur.

Section Five
What's Next In This Process?

Chapter 11

Publishing, Marketing, And Beyond

The starting point of all achievement is desire.
~ Napoleon Hill

Now it's time to get back to the marketing of your book and the expanding of your foundation for ongoing prosperity. Think of your book as simply one piece of the funnel that you will create as part of this business model. The pieces of your funnel may include a free giveaway, an e-course, an evergreen product, additional products, a live online course, a home study course, a membership course, mentoring or consulting, and a live event.

When you create a book, you actually create an experience, and these funnel components are the experience unfolding over time. The ultimate experience is your live event where people are able to spend time with you face to face in an organized setting, but allow them to enjoy the experience of learning from you and absorbing your knowledge through everything else I am describing here. I will discuss each of these in great detail here, but first let's get back to the basics of how you will get your name and message out to the world to begin with.

First, remember the promise of this book. It was to teach you how to:

Write. Publish. Prosper.

Write Prolifically.
Publish Globally.
Prosper Eternally.

- ✓ Write/Create...Books, Blogs, Live Courses, Home Study courses, Information Products, Videos, Audios, Live Events
- ✓ Publish...Online (Digital) and In Print (Physical)
- ✓ Prosper...Build a Substantial, Ongoing Income from Multiple Streams

Book, Blog, and Podcast

The foundation of what I am teaching is based upon you having a blog, a book, and also a podcast to begin with. This three-pronged approach is one that continues to serve me very well as my business grows.

You are already writing your book with help from me here.

Your hosted WordPress site is next – make sure you are posting *at least* once a week on a topic closely related to your book. Don't allow the technology of setting up your site hold you back or cause you any delay in achieving your goals; tech people are plentiful and the cost is relatively low.

Creating content does not have to be a struggle. You can write some of your own posts, use private label rights (PLR) content for others, and invite people to write guest posts for your blog as well.

Podcast on iTunes – use the free Pod Press plugin on your blog to add your audio there. Think of podcasting as simply recording your ideas for twenty or thirty minutes, either on your own or as an interview with someone else. I've now produced about a hundred and twenty podcast episodes and love this method of getting my information and training out to the world.

I have included details on all of this in the *Resources* section at the end of this book.

Your Marketing Funnel

There is no right or wrong way to set up your marketing funnel. In fact, I flipped the funnel on its side when I wrote this book. I decided to teach the Write. Publish. Prosper. course as a live online training first to my high level mentoring students. Then I wrote this book to set my marketing funnel into motion.

Let's look at each of these pieces I have mentioned previously much more closely.

Free Giveaway – The primary purpose of your free giveaway (also referred to as an 'ethical bribe') is to encourage and persuade a visitor to your site to exchange their name and email address for what you are offering them when they join your permission based list. This must be something irresistible!

Remember why they may be interested in you and your topic and prepare something for them that will take them from where they are right now to closer to where they want to be. Over the years I have found that written and audio content are the most appealing, but you will want to experiment with different giveaways to see which ones work best for you and your topic within your target audience. Think about putting together worksheets, checklists, or a short report on a specific aspect of your topic, or to create an audio recording that shares important information to the listener.

The idea is to convert someone from a visitor into a prospect as quickly as possible, assuming they will benefit from their connection with you and get closer to achieving their own goals as a result of what you will share with them. My final advice on this is to keep it simple!

5 or 7 Part E-course – I'm not sure exactly why this is, but a 5 or 7 day e-course seems to work best. Set it up in your autoresponder to be delivered every day, or at least every other day so prospects will get the information quickly and evenly. Throughout your e-course, provide readers with a link to the entire e-course at least a couple of times. That way if they do not receive one of your emails, or accidentally delete it, they will still have access to the entire e-course you put together. The idea here is to reach people using something referred to as the 'Zeigarnik Effect'.

Bluma Wulfovna Zeigarnik was a Russian psychologist who specialized in human behavior. After years of study she came up with the theory that states that people remember uncompleted or interrupted tasks better than completed tasks. The 'Zeigarnik Effect' suggests that students who suspend their study, during which they do unrelated activities, will remember material better than students who complete study sessions without a break. This means that people will respond more positively and retain more of what you share over a period of time with them in these short mini-lessons than they would if you simply provided it for them all at once in the format of an eBook or short report.

Let readers know something is for sale by providing links within your lessons. Be sure to include a 'CTA' (call to action) on the final day of your e-course to let them know how they can work with you further. Be creative with this!

In the *Resources* section at the end of this book I have included a 7 Day E-Course on the topic of getting organized and decluttering for entrepreneurs. It is my hope that this completed e-course serve as a guideline for what you will prepare for your own niche topic.

'Flagship' or 'Signature' Product - Based on the response and feedback you receive over time from your free giveaway,

this will lead you organically to your first product. Think of this as your 'flagship' or 'signature' product or course that you will be known for as your business grows. I recommend that this be an 'evergreen' digital product, meaning that you will not need to change or update it significantly for at least three years. Stay away from products based on technology here, as that tends to change very rapidly. You don't want to create a popular product that is obsolete within months.

The fastest and easiest products can be created by teaching someone else what you know about a topic. Spend time reading and researching this topic and you will know more than ninety percent of the people who are seeking more information about it. I like to do a webinar or series of teleseminars where I go into detail about a topic. That webinar or teleseminar then becomes the basis of the product, with either a Study Guide, transcription, or checklists to round it out. If you use the webinar format, be sure to provide an audio (mp3) of it so your customers can listen to it again without having to watch the webinar again if they choose not to. Convenience is key to successful products.

How to Create Your First Product

I'd like to address the idea of creating a product right here and now. Over these past nine years I have seen people struggle over how to create their own digital information products, and even I took a full year to create my first product after coming online because I was stuck in the how and what when it comes to product creation. It doesn't have to be so difficult.

Look back at the products and courses you have purchased since getting involved with writing, marketing, and entrepreneurship. If you are like most people, you have a plethora of products residing on your hard drive, and yet may not have gone through any of them fully.

If you can, find the original email and sales letter that led to you being interested enough in the product in order to purchase it. Does it still sound like what you thought it would be, now that some time has passed? What was the promise, expressed or implied, given by the product creator that convinced you to buy?

Once you can figure out the answers to these questions you will be on your way to successful product creation.

First, you want to uncover a need in your niche market. The best products come from you having an unmet need and figuring out a way to solve it. For example, I saw that no one was teaching a complete course on how to effectively write, publish, and market books in the non-fiction genre. I did quite a bit of research, purchased many people's products on how to do this, and came to the conclusion that there was definitely a need for this type of training. Many people agree, and that's how I have sold so many courses to people around the world.

Start small. Choose just one aspect of the problem you wish to solve with your product. Like I mentioned in the previous section, you will present your training via a teleseminar or webinar if that is appropriate. Make some notes and turn them into a Study Guide.

My very first product, created in the fall of 2006, was a series of four teleseminars on how to write articles and blog posts to get your business off the ground. It was based on my experiences during the previous two or three months in learning how to write effectively for my business and drive traffic to my sites, all while building my list. I included a Study Guide in PDF format so the students could print it out, make their own notes, and then take action on what I had taught them. The teleseminars were all available as mp3 downloads or streaming on their own computer (I've included a link in the *Resources* section to the service I continue to use for this purpose, as well as for both of my podcasts).

As soon as you have the idea for your product and have done the research to make sure it is a viable one, give your product a name and purchase the domain for it. I will not go into a detailed discussion here about choosing and purchasing domains, so suffice it to say that whatever you choose will be perfectly acceptable for this first product.

Add this domain to your hosting service, and then install WordPress (or have the tech person you will be using do this for you). Your site is now set up and ready for you to complete your product. You will have a sales letter, a thank you page, a download page (or member's area), and a page to offer additional products of your own or affiliate products that are related to and relevant for your target market. When you think of it in this way, as a site consisting of four or five pages, it simplifies what you may have thought was going to be extremely complicated.

The next step is to actually create the product. It won't be excellent the first time out, but you must get started so you will have something tangible to improve upon. Remember that you can and will update your product, and if you learn something new it is a simple process to add the additional information to your download page or member's area. It gets much faster and easier each time, and soon you will wonder why it took you so long to start creating products that others will benefit from.

Additional Digital Products – These will flow naturally once you get your first one out there, and be sure to do the market research on the demand for what you have in mind rather than listening to what a few people tell you they would like. I know people who spend weeks or months creating products that do not sell, only because a handful of people told them they were interested in learning about that topic. Sometimes, even those people who said they wanted it in the first place do not buy the completed product, and that can be quite frustrating.

Live Online Course - The next logical step is to create a live online course that you deliver over a period of four to six sessions. I have done this at least twenty times since coming online, and truly enjoy the immediate feedback and interaction with my students that only a live course can offer.

I start out by making notes on what I want to teach, and then create a PowerPoint in order to deliver the concepts in a sequential and organized way. I prefer four sessions of about sixty to ninety minutes each, presented weekly. You may also want to add a Question and Answer session at the end that can be hosted as a teleseminar.

Home Study Course - After you teach your online course one time, immediately put it into a Home Study format. This is more in line with the concept of creating multiple income streams, where you do not need to be there in order to earn income. I still like to teach live, but it is a choice and not because my business model requires me to do it.

If you do not wish to teach your online course live again after the first time, simply host teleseminars every few months to address questions and concerns and to keep the course current. This will boost sales over time as people see the value they are receiving from the additional help you are giving them in this way.

Membership Sites - These are an excellent way to flesh out your marketing funnel and connect with a larger community. These are perfect no matter what your niche, and I work personally with people doing this in the area of horse training and care, embroidery as a business, training virtual assistants, reflexology, and so many more. You must commit to adding valuable and relevant content as a regular basis, and to building relationships with your members to address their needs and concerns. They will tell you exactly which products you should create next, and this is invaluable to you as an entrepreneur.

At some point people will ask you about coaching or mentoring them. You must decide if this will be a part of your business model or not, as it requires you to be available on a regular basis to talk with each person individually or within a small group. I used to work with as many as twenty-five mentees individually, and more than two hundred in a group setting. Over time I decided to drastically change this model. I ended my small group mentoring at the end of 2013 and now only work individually with about a dozen people each year.

Another part of my business is consulting work for companies and corporations. I'll write about this in more detail in the final chapter of this book.

I will also share my experiences in hosting live events in the next chapter. Do not be afraid of getting in front of people to share your ideas and knowledge. I had terrible stage fright when I first came online and that's why being a part of Rotary and other charitable organizations was good for me. I got used to holding the microphone and speaking in front of groups and the fear dissipated over time. Now you can't get the microphone away from me!

The Product Line Funnel Model

Now I would like to present a model for a product line funnel for your business. This is different from your marketing funnel in that I am listing and describing the products you will want to create over time. This model has worked extremely well for me and for the hundreds of other successful authors, publishers, and entrepreneurs I have connected with during my nine years of being online. This is how it goes:

✓ Start with a high value, front end product that is specific to your topic. This would sell for less than thirty dollars and would be in the format of a short (fewer than fifty pages) eBook, an audio or video series, or a one hour recorded webinar training. Provides a complete solution to one problem. It is a high quality product, and includes related high quality bonuses (ask others for these when you are just getting started). This is typically the first product a customer will buy from you. Even though it is intended to be a low entry product, your goal is to impress people with the quality and value of what you are offering. Your goal is to introduce people to who you are and what you do as a stepping stone to your other products, courses, and programs. This front end product can be sold directly from your blog.

✓ The next offering could be a subscription that you offer monthly. Think of having an audio or video series, a physical CD or print newsletter, an email course, or even software that you have created for you. This is a logical upsell to your front end product and would sell for less than thirty dollars a month. This ongoing training would offer more help to solve the same problems, but offers unique value that is different from the front end product. I prefer to offer this as a 'fixed term' subscription and your prospect/client would complete it in about six months.

✓ Next comes your 'flagship' or 'signature' product that I outlined above. Again, you are always creating information products of the highest value and quality, and remember to keep updating them as needed when there are changes to your topic or you learn or discover something additional that is relevant. This would sell for about a hundred dollars.

✓ A membership site could follow, but be aware that this will take lots of your time. I shared earlier that I had over two hundred people in a monthly mentoring program for several years. Finally it was taking too much of my time and I ended it in December of 2014. Some of the members have continued to work with me in my Platinum Mastermind Mentor program, and others remain as subscribers to my list. The monthly cost for this would vary, depending upon what you will be offering to your members.

✓ Your 'BIG' course or program is the next logical step. This is the course I describe above when I discuss having a live, online training that runs for four to six weeks.

✓ Coaching, consulting, and mentoring come next, and this can be extremely lucrative.

✓ Hosting your own live events rounds out this product line funnel.

Now we will move on to the next steps that will get you even closer to your goal of writing, publishing, and prospering as a business model.

Chapter 12

Taking It to the Next Level

Always bear in mind that your own resolution to succeed is
more important than any other.
~ Abraham Lincoln

As you will see, writing your book and publishing it for the world is just the tip of the iceberg as to what is possible with this business model. Where you go from here is completely up to you, but know that becoming a published author is the first step in attaining the confidence you need to pursue higher endeavors.

We must all prepare for the stages of our life. There will come a time when you want to do things differently in your business, and if you have set the proper elements in place it will be a smooth transition over time. You may be aware of actors who seem to disappear after being in a popular movie or television series, while others are around for decades. The ones who thought ahead and formed production companies, became producers, writers, or directors, and surrounded themselves with other talented artists are the ones who thrive. You will do the same as your business grows and you mature and change your desires for the lifestyle you wish to live. You and I are 'works in progress' as human beings, authors, and entrepreneurs. Prepare for your masterpiece in a way that pleases you the most.

Write. Publish. Prosper.

I'll be sharing the next logical steps with you here, which in my way of thinking include speaking engagements, coaching and consulting, and hosting your own virtual and live events. But first, let's discuss taking your book to bestseller status.

Thinking of Yourself as a Publisher

It was a difficult leap for me to think of myself as an author, but the biggest hurdle in my thinking was when I went from that to thinking of myself as a publisher. Yet this is exactly what you want to do in order to build a lucrative business based on your book.

The first time I introduced myself as a publisher was in 2012 at a charity fundraising event in Santa Barbara. I had just had some new business cards made that had my name, the name of my publishing company (Hunter's Moon Publishing), and the title of 'Author – Publisher – Entrepreneur'.

Eyes widened, conversation stopped, and suddenly the people around me had questions about what I was doing in my business. I then went on to share some of what I am including here in this book. When people ask you detailed questions about what you are doing, you know you're on the right track towards success.

Remember that when you create a book you are creating an experience for your readers and followers. Therefore, spending time in person with these people is like bringing your book to life. Think about someone you admire, perhaps an author, actor, humanitarian, thought leader, or sports figure. Imagine being able to spend some time with them face to face, asking them your questions and learning more about them. Wouldn't that be worth your time and money to do so? That's exactly the way many people will feel about you as you begin to make a name for yourself by sharing your thoughts, ideas, knowledge, and experiences on your topic with the world.

I was first spoke at a marketing conference back in 2008 when Matt Bacak asked me to be one of the presenters at his 'Marketing Madness' event in Atlanta. I was flattered and couldn't wait to be on the stage in front of his large group and to share the stage with some of the biggest names in marketing at that time. It was a disaster for me, but I learned much from this experience.

The reason my presentation was not very good (okay, it was awful!) was that I had no platform or unique perspective on my topic of online marketing. Even though I had reached six figures a year in earnings by this time I was not memorable. I did sell a few of my programs from the stage that day, so you can still make some money as a speaker even when you are not adequately prepared, but it is not the most enjoyable way to build a sustainable business.

After I spoke that day I went to lunch with my mentor, Raymond Aaron. Coincidentally, Raymond was speaking at this same event, and it was wonderful to be able to have this time with him to hear his critique of the information I had just delivered. He basically told me that I needed to have a Mission and a Vision for my niche topic and that I needed to spend time laying a foundation and building a platform before I spoke again. Sound familiar?

Within a week I had revamped my main blog, ConnieRagenGreen.com, started a new blog at HugeProfitsTinyList.com, and began thinking seriously about the book I would write. Within a few months I had also added Armand Morin as a mentor and my business began to fall into place. It would take a year and a half more for me to write and publish my book, but you do not need to wait that long now that you have this training available on how to do it quickly.

Speaking Engagements

You must actively go after speaking engagements at venues where your target market will show up. Sometimes event promoters will come to you, as Matt Bacak did with me years ago and several others have done since, but you must not count on that. Instead, reach out to the people who are hosting live conferences and workshops and offer to do a presentation on your topic at their next event. Even if they don't take you up on your offer, they will begin to watch what you are doing to see how you might work together in the future.

Their first step may be to have you as a guest on a webinar, to ask you to write a guest post for their blog, or to interview you for their podcast. I recommend reaching out to them first, and inviting them to write a guest post for you or to be a guest on your podcast. These actions on your part will definitely get their attention.

Eventually you will become known for your topic and be asked to speak at various venues. This will then put you in the position of being able to pick and choose where you will speak and under what circumstances. Over the years I have changed the way I choose the events I will speak at, and this is based primarily on the reputation of the promoter and of the event itself.

I prefer to not be paid to speak and to pay all of my own expenses to travel to the location of the event and to stay in the hotel. Instead, at the end of my presentation I am able to offer one of my packages. This is referred to as 'selling from the stage', and typically the promoter takes half of what you sell.

Do not forget that hosting your own teleseminars and webinars is also public speaking. Do these regularly and you will always have content ready to share at someone else's event. This business model is quite effective in leveraging your time as you earn a substantial income.

Another thing I will mention here is that you always want to be prepared. Keep a copy of one or two of your presentations with you at all time, either on a portable drive, in your Dropbox account, or as an email attachment. Many times you will attend an event and one of the speakers is unable to go on. Being prepared with a relevant presentation will save the day for the promoter of the event and give you an opportunity you may not have had otherwise.

Coaching/Consulting/Mentoring

When I was first asked to come into a company and help them with their marketing I was intimidated. It was my belief that I was not the person to best help them and I even said as much to the CEO. He insisted that I was the perfect person to help his company, so I made an appointment and showed up.

It was a wonderful experience and now I can't imagine this type of work not being a part of my business model. I keep this to no more than three days each month of being at these places in person, and most of what I do with them is done by webinar. I help companies and corporations of various sizes with social media management, email marketing strategies, content creation, and more.

It was my connection with the non-profit world that landed me that first client and led me to others. I had built a reputation of integrity, strong work ethic, and goals driven, something they valued immensely. If you are a part of your local Chamber of Commerce this may be another way to become known locally.

If this is an area you may be interested in pursuing, contact some local corporations and ask them if they are open to having you come in for a two hour presentation on your topic to a segment of their employees. Let them know more about you and send them the information they request as a way to get your foot in the door.

Hosting Your Own Live Events

The first event I ever hosted was at a small theatre in Santa Clarita in 2007. Several business leaders from the community had asked me to share some thoughts on the topic of marketing online with other small business owners.

About twenty-five people showed up that day, and I was hooked on sharing and teaching in front of a group. Even though many of them had been in business for more than thirty years, I was perceived as the expert when it came to marketing a business on the Internet.

Some time passed before I decided to host my own events. I was being asked to speak more regularly all over the United States and it just didn't seem necessary to take the time and incur the expense of hosting my own events if I was being given multiple opportunities to speak for others. Then, during the next couple of years I spoke at events where I was not satisfied with how everything was handled. Instead of complaining, I made the decision to host my own events.

Because I will still relatively new to all of this I asked my friend and colleague Dr. Jeanette Cates if we do one live event together. Jeanette had hosted her own events for many years and agreed to do one with me.

We called it the Online Revenue Workshop, and we ended up holding five of these over a period of about two and a half years. The first four were in Las Vegas and the final one was held in Austin, Texas. I learned so much from these experiences that I was finally ready to do one on my own.

In the fall of 2013 I hosted the first of the Weekend Marketer Live workshop events, based on my bestselling book of the same name and my online course. Two more followed, and in October of 2014 I announced that my next live events would be slightly different.

In March of 2015 I'll be hosting the first Write. Publish. Prosper. live event in Los Angeles, California.

All of my events are 'workshop' style, meaning that students actually get some work done while they are at the event. I also refer to them as 'boutique' workshops, meaning that I only take a maximum of forty people each time.

I would encourage you to reread this chapter and come up with a strategy you will implement in order to take your new business to the next level over this next year.

Conclusion

If not us, then who?
If not now, then when?
~ John E. Lewis

It is my sincere hope that you can now see how the process of writing and publishing your book, as well as creating an entire business based on your topic is one that will be worthwhile to you. Finding your voice and sharing your message with the world in this way will empower you to achieve any goals you have set for yourself. I know you now have the tools to start this challenge and change your life.

Summoning Up the Courage

The only question then becomes:

'Will you have the courage to do what it takes to write and publish a book and build an empire based on what you wish to share about your topic?'

The life of the author and entrepreneur is one of independence and industriousness. It allows you to control and change your destiny.

I believe that anyone can turn themselves into an entrepreneur, even if that is not something that was previously in your line of thinking. It is natural to want independence in our lives, to be hard working and industrious, and to be goal-oriented. Your perspective may be different than mine, and that is dependent upon your upbringing.

If this is all very new to you, think about gaining a new perspective and framework in order to succeed. This is achieved by committing to further study, ongoing reading, and taking action on the steps I have shared in this book.

Choosing to Begin

It all starts when you choose to begin. Taking that first step on the path to writing and publishing your book and then turning it all into a business may be a scary one, but I promise that it will soon become second nature to you.

Think of this book as a resource guide and blueprint for the business you want to create. As an entrepreneur, your path will be unique and will require you to take a leap of faith more than once as you progress. Know that you can do whatever you want to do, and that the only way to fail is by refusing to take any action at all.

Get into the habit of moving forward every single day, with conviction and at all costs. Refuse to be dissuaded by others or by that 'little voice' in your head. Resolve to finish what you stat, and congratulate yourself at every turn. You are a special and unique human being who deserves to be celebrated.

Share your successes, however small they may be in the beginning, and show an honest enthusiasm for your work when doing so. This will be the way to creating a life and a business where you can write prolifically, publish globally, and prosper eternally.

Appendix A

7 Day E-Course Example

7 Days to a DeCluttered Home Office in 10 Minutes a Day

Day 1 –

Subject Line:
[Day 1] firstname, your decluttering e-course

Welcome to your E-Course '7 Days to a DeCluttered Home Office in 10 Minutes a Day'. Today is Day 1, so be prepared to think about organization in a whole new way.

First, take some pictures of your home office work space from various angles. It will be much easier to tackle clutter when you can visualize what needs to be done.

Next, make a list of the items that need to be straightened up and organized, as well as the specific areas that need your attention immediately.

Finally, decide how and where you will

store the items you will be saving. I've discovered in helping so many people organize their clutter over the years that proper storage is an integral part of the process.

Tomorrow we'll take a look at where to begin and then dive right in!

To Getting Organized Once and For All!
Your Name

Day 2 -

Subject Line:
[Day 2] firstname, pictures of your home office

Did you take pictures of your home office to see more clearly what needs to be thrown away, straightened up, and organized in a way that works for you?

It's a good idea to have these pictures so you'll be able to see how far you've come at the end of your 7 Day E-Course. Look at the list you started yesterday. There may be a specific area or group of items that scream out to you...

'Organize me first!'

This might be a book shelf, piles of papers or magazines on the floor or directly adjacent to your desk work area, or perhaps the table where your printer sits. If so, spend just 10 minutes today going through these and sorting into 3 piles...

1) To be gone through more thoroughly

2) To save & store neatly

3) To throw into the trash!

Now, throw away the trash, put the items you are saving into a corner where you will be able to get to them easily when you are ready to store them, and begin going through the final pile to see what you will save, give away, shred, or toss into the trash.

Are you beginning to see that this is a doable challenge?

To Getting Organized Once and For All!
Your Name

Day 3 -

Subject Line:
[Day 3] firstname, how will I store it all?

By this time you may be thinking that you want to save and store more items than you thought. If that is the case, then you will need boxes, plastic or other types of storage containers, and additional shelving (going UP is a great alternative to expanding OUT, don't you think?)

I've put together a list of items you will want to take a look at for this purpose. You can pick them up at the big box stores and discount stores in your city, or order them directly from Amazon and have them delivered to your doorstep.

http://connieLoves.me/GetOrganized (This is an active link for your reference)

Spend ten minutes today making sure you have the right boxes, containers, and shelving for all of your storage needs.

To Getting Organized Once and For All! Your Name

Day 4 -

Subject Line:
[Day 4] firstname, let's dig in!

Today we're going to roll up our sleeves and start the decluttering process in a big way. Choose just one area (drawer, section of your desk, pile of things on the floor (I'm not calling it junk!) and start sorting out the good, the bad, and the not so pretty.

While you do this, take a look at some
of the videos on my YouTube Channel I
have prepared for you to make it easier
and more fun to get organized...

http://www.youtube.com/watch?v=VNZ9fcwb_9A

To Getting Organized Once and For All!
Your Name

P.S. Pick up this entire 7 Day E-Course
as a PDF download at no cost at:

http://yoursite.com/7dayecourse

Day 5 -

Subject Line:
[Day 5] firstname, I wrote the book on decluttering

Did you know that I wrote a book on the
topic of getting organized and decluttering
your home office? Well, I did and I believe
my book could be extremely helpful to you.
Pick it up here in paperback or as a Kindle
version to get started right away.

http://linktoyourbook.com

Today you'll spend 10 minutes tackling the
clutter on the floor of your home office.
If you're like most people who work from
home, anything you intend to get to later
ends up on the floor.

Choose a medium sized pile and dig in, and remember your goal is to divide it up into 3 new piles - one that you are saving and storing, another to go through completely within the next 24 hours, and a final one to throw away for good.

To Getting Organized Once and For All!
Your Name

Day 6 -

Subject Line:
[Day 6] firstname, some helpful tips for you

Congratulations on getting through the first five days of decluttering and organizing your home office work area!

Before we go any further I want to give you some tips for having a pleasing and desirable area to work productively and effectively from each day.

1) Draw a floor plan to decide where you will place your office furniture

2) Including shelving, as going UP is much better than expanding OUT

3) Make sure closets and filing cabinets have enough room to open easily

4) Include natural light in your office

5) Commit to spending ten minutes every
day eliminating clutter that builds up

Today you'll spend ten minutes sitting
at your desk and looking for any areas
that need to be decluttered immediately.
If you desk space is already clear, open
the closet and get to work!

To Getting Organized Once and For All!
Your Name

P.S. Pick up this entire 7 Day E-Course
as a PDF download at no cost at:

http://yoursite.com/7dayecourse

Day 7 -

Subject Line:
[Day 7] firstname, look what you have accomplished!

Hopefully by now you are seeing a major
change in the look and feel of your home
office. Isn't it amazing how much you
can accomplish in five or ten minutes
a day?

Be sure to take pictures and compare
them to the ones you took on the first
day of this e-course. Quite a dramatic
change, don't you agree?

Now it's time to think about your next
steps in the game of decluttering. You
already know that I'm an author and an

expert in this field, but did you know that I also have a popular product that is an advanced training on how to get organized in all areas of your life? It is called:

'Organize Your Home and Your Life'?

This is a course that provides a step by step blueprint for eliminating clutter from your home and work space while also helping you to clear your mind, get more focused on your goals, and take action to live the life you deserve.

Find out more at:

http://yoursite.com

Also, I'd love to hear from you about what you learned most from this 7 day e-course and what else would help you to move forward in your life and your business. Simply hit 'reply' and talk to me.

To Getting Organized Once and For All!
Your Name

P.S. Pick up this entire 7 Day E-Course as a PDF download at no cost at:

http://yoursite.com/7dayecourse

Free Giveaway Example

This is the Special Report I offer when people come to one of my opt in pages:

Your Online Entrepreneur Blueprint;
11 Steps To Entrepreneurial Success

What does it take to become a successful online entrepreneur today?

That's the question I am often asked, and I feel uniquely qualified to answer it in great detail for you.

My name is Connie Ragen Green, and I first came online at the end of 2005. I had been working for most of the previous 20 years as a classroom teacher in the Los Angeles area, teaching all the way from Kindergarten through high school. My favorite grades to teach were 5th and 6th, because I felt like I related to that age group in a special way. They were at the point in their lives where they needed an adult role model to help guide them to their future. Also, they 'got' my jokes, allowing for an open learning environment in which young minds could receive knowledge and expand.

At the same time I was also working as a real estate broker and residential appraiser. I did this after school, on weekends, and during school breaks and vacations. I had worked in real estate for several years in my 20s before returning to school to earn my teaching credential, and loved helping people to find a new home or sell the one they had, and to receive a fair price for it. The additional income was also important to me, as everyone knows that school teachers do not earn enough money to buy a home, especially in southern California. My appraisal work took me from my home at that time in the San Fernando Valley section of Los Angeles to as far south as San Diego, east to Palm Springs, and as far north as Santa Barbara, and even further at times. Sometimes I would put a thousand miles on my car within the course of a single week.

By 2005 I was exhausted from working six or seven days a week for the past twenty years, with only a few short real vacations during that time. Perhaps the most difficult part of these was that I was still living month to month, with no hope of getting ahead financially. I'm also a cancer survivor, so I knew that my life had to hold more meaning than to simply spend it working at jobs I no longer had a passion for. When I discovered that people were making a living on the Internet with information products, affiliate marketing, and online training I knew this was for me.

The question I had to ask myself was this: "Am I willing to do what it takes to become an online entrepreneur?"

That was in December of 2005. I set about to see if I could start an online business, or if this was something others could be successful at but not me. My belief system at that time included the feeling that everyone else was smarter than I was, had a stronger background in whatever I was trying to achieve, and simply knew things that I did not. Over the next six months to a year I was tested time and time again as I worked hard to put the pieces in place. There was no boss or supervisor checking to see what I had done each day. I earned no money in the very beginning, yet I was having to spend money on domains, web hosting, the teleseminar service, and an autoresponder account. Would it all be worth it?

The answer was a resounding Yes! And now I teach others how to get started with their own Internet businesses.

Becoming an entrepreneur of any type is simply not for everyone. If you are used to having a traditional schedule, weekends off, and a regular paycheck you may not care for having your own business. If, on the other hand, you look forward to being in charge and making decisions, having the opportunity to earn as much as you want to, and love taking risks on a daily basis, entrepreneurship could be exactly what suits you best.

In order to build up a successful business online you must be willing to do what it takes. This means setting up a quiet workspace for yourself at home, scheduling the days and times you will be at work, creating content for your blog and websites, and connecting with others both online and in person. Of course, this is after you have chosen a niche in which to specialize and made sure it is one that will hold your interest for at least the next year. I'll be going into great detail with each of these areas when we discuss the 11 steps to entrepreneurial success.

You must also find out what your competition is already selling to this market. Competition is to be respected because this means that people are ready, willing, and able to spend money on a variety of products and services. Join the list of everyone who is currently serving your market to see what they have to say, and become an affiliate for them if they have such a program.

Now it is time for you to make a name for yourself in your chosen niche. Blog as often as possible and say what you think. It's better to be controversial and speak your mind than to be wishy-washy and go along with everyone else. Read everything you can on your topic, and not just from online sources. Visit your public library and bookstores. See what you already may have on your bookshelves at home. Focus on becoming as knowledgeable as you possibly can on your niche topic, as this is the path to becoming an expert or authority.

The final piece is marketing your new online business, and that's the glue to keeping it all together. I like to market every single day, even weekends and holidays because it makes my business stronger and increases my income. Remember that a single tweet on Twitter is marketing, and that much of your online marketing can be automated, so it's not like you'll be sitting in front of your computer six or seven days a week.

Have fun with the marketing and it will serve you well. Send out email messages to the people who join your list, including links to your blog posts, affiliate offers, and excellent resources. Be active on the 'Big Three' social media sites (Facebook, Twitter, and LinkedIn) and share your blog posts and other content there as well. It won't be long before you are thought of as an authority in your niche, and your online business begins to skyrocket. Doing what it takes is your key to success.

As I stated earlier, it took me almost a year to start making a decent amount of money online. I had made a few hundred dollars during the first six months, but it was hit and miss and barely paid my expenses for hosting, autoresponders, and domains. I believe it was due to the fact that I did not have the 11 steps I will be sharing with you here in place in my own online business. If I had known then what I know now, things would have been very different.

Instead of taking 18 months to replace my offline income, I could have done it in 6 to 9 months. I have included the 11 steps to starting your online business in the order they should be done. You can do this in as little as thirty days, but most people will spend at least two to three months to get started. Take it at your own pace, and don't omit any steps.

Let's get started!

11 Steps To Entrepreneurial Success; Based on My Experiences and Those Of My Own Students

Step #1 – Change Your Mindset

Thinking about your life is a matter of choice. Earlier I said that my belief system before I became an entrepreneur included the feeling that everyone else was smarter than I was, had a stronger background in whatever I was trying to achieve, and simply knew things that I did not. It took time for me to understand there was no truth in that whatsoever. Know that you are capable of great things and that you can activate that part of your mind's thinking at any time.

I used to engage in negative self-talk every single day of my life. Once I began to focus on the positive aspects of who I was I could look into the mirror every morning and say something to the effect of 'You are smart and have knowledge and information that will change other people's lives forever.' Now I can't imagine not feeling empowered in this way, but it did take some time to get to this point in my life. Being positive will meet with some resistance from those in your life you are steeped in negativity and self-doubt, but do not allow them to dictate your future. Practice positive self-talk every day and you will be amazed at the results.

Step #2 – Choose a Profitable Niche

Deciding what you have to offer others is sometimes the most difficult step of all. My advice is to choose an area you are interested in and know something about, and then jump in and get started. You may find that the first niche you choose does not hold your interest forever, but you must begin somewhere in order to get started with this process. Take a close look at your work experience in previous years, hobbies, and other areas of interest to you.

Think of a three circle Venn diagram that you might remember from school. I use it to help my coaching clients choose a niche that is right for them. Recently I worked with someone who is an embroidery coach. She's been involved in embroidery since she was very young, and knows quite a bit about this topic. When we worked on this together she saw that she is passionate about helping others to start and grow an embroidery business, has lots of life experience in this area, and the market is definitely in place. Tens of thousands of people around the world are into embroidery, or want to get started with it. She is now on her way to online success and has already achieved great things.

Some of the most popular niches include:
- Health and Fitness
- Relationships
- Make Money/Save Time
- DIY Home Improvement

Write. Publish. Prosper.

- Sports/Hobbies
- Family/Lifestyle/Choices
- Self Improvement/Personal Growth
- Becoming an Author

These are just a few examples of where you may want to start out with your online business.

Step #3 - Choose a Profitable Business Model

I have had up to eight streams of online income since starting my business at the beginning of 2006. These days I focus on just a few of these, but I wanted to make sure you knew about every possible way to earn money as an online entrepreneur. These business models include:

- Services – Take a look at the skills you have previously acquired, what you already know how to do, and which of these can be done from home. This could include transcribing, editing, setting up websites, graphic design, customer service, being a virtual assistant for one or more people, and more. You will find that there are thousands of people like myself who hire independent contractors to help us with our businesses. I have a dozen people who assist me in some capacity, and they are an integral part of my team. Being in service can be a lucrative and rewarding way to get started as an online entrepreneur.

- Local Business Marketing – I kind of fell into this business model by offering to help a family member who had just started a handyman business. He was spending so much money on newspaper and magazine advertising that it would take him a couple of weeks each month just to get to the 'break even' point. I offered to help him in 2006 by using a blog and other online marketing techniques I was learning and within two months he had dropped the other advertising completely because he was getting so many calls.

  Soon my insurance agent and dentist asked me to help them with their local marketing and on my way to a live event the following year I met two plumbers who hired me while we were at thirty thousand feet in the air! This continues to be an excellent business model.

- Affiliate Marketing – This is the process of recommending other people's products and services in return for a commission. Affiliate marketing continues to account for about half of my income each month, and I only recommend what I have purchased, consumed, and benefited from. I even wrote a book about it called *Huge Profits With Affiliate Marketing: How to Build an Online Empire by Recommending What*

You Love. I go into much greater detail with all of the ways you can build a profitable business by being an affiliate for others.

- Information Product Creation – Creating your own line of products will serve you well over time. I started with simple courses that consisted of three or four live teleseminars with recordings, transcripts, and Study Guides. Other products consist of a written guide in PDF (portable document format) and a few short videos. These courses become evergreen products you can sell online for years to come. You then set up an affiliate program so that others can promote you and your products the way you do when you are the affiliate.

  Keep your products simple and create them as quickly as possible for best results. A great example of this is a course that I created with one of my students, Adrienne Dupree. It's at http://TopWPPluginsForBusiness.com and is only $7.

- Membership Sites – Everyone loves to feel like they belong to a group, so you can set up membership sites to include your products and other information. Then you sell a monthly, annual, or lifetime subscription to your site and continue to add to your training as you bring in new members. This has become super simple in recent years thanks to an inexpensive plugin for

WordPress called Wishlist. I now have many membership sites of all kinds and find it to be the easiest way to increase my income while building my online business. You can find out more about the Wishlist plugin at http://ConnieLoves.me/Wishlist.

- Niche Sites – If you're truly having fun with your Internet business then you'll want to expand into other niches for fun and profit. This is where I first began including close friends and family members in what I was doing online. Choose topics of interest like cooking, skateboarding, or travel and set up a simple WordPress site. There's an entire strategy to this that includes using PLR (private label rights) content and promoting products through an affiliate link for Amazon, Clickbank, or other programs and even adding some AdSense blocks to further monetize your site.

- Authorship/Speaking/Consulting – I didn't even think of this as a business model until I wrote my first book in 2010. Even though I had been speaking at marketing events for a couple of years by then it was when I was first published that I saw the lucrative possibilities of writing, speaking, and consulting. You can see how I've done this by visiting my Author's Page on Amazon at http://ConnieRagenGreenBooks.com.

- Coaching/Mentoring – I highly recommend that you achieve some success yourself before offering to help others. You want to have a certain level of credibility, and I waited until I had reached six figures a year at the end of 2007 before starting my Mentor Program. This accounts for only about ten percent of my overall income because my time is precious and I prefer to work with fewer people on a one to one basis.

By now you can see that there are quite a few business models to pursue as an online entrepreneur. Start with one or two to begin with and see where that strategy leads you.

Step #4 Purchase Your Domains And Hosting

Next, you will want to purchase your domain names and hosting. If you do not yet have your name as a dot come, as I do with both ConnieGreen.com and ConnieRagenGreen.com, do that first. If your name is not available you'll want to choose a middle name or initial to claim your name online. Someone had ConnieGreen.com already when I got started, so I put a backorder on it and was able to pick it up the following year. This will be the most important domain you own, so purchase it for five years or longer.

Your other sites will need their own domains. Start with one other one to set up your business. Choose a domain name that says what you will be doing online. Remember that you are just starting out, so don't worry about choosing the perfect domain name. Shorter is better – three or four words – and you will be better off with a .com than with any other extension.

Your domain must live somewhere so that you can quickly install a WordPress site. For hosting, I recommend http://BlueHostSolutions.com (this is my affiliate link). This is what is referred to as C-panel hosting, and this service allows you to add Wordpress in just a few clicks so that you will be ready to start blogging. The cost for this is less than one hundred dollars for an entire year. You can have up to 100 domains with just one account, so it is extremely cost effective. I do NOT recommend using GoDaddy for your hosting because they are not equipped with C-panel and you will run into problems almost immediately as you start your online business.

Step #5 – Set Up A WordPress Blog/Site

When I was just starting out, Wordpress seemed too confusing for me. It was very technical. Now it is much easier to do because it has become user friendly. You will install Wordpress on your domain with just a few clicks through your hosting account.

Now you will want to add a new theme to your blog. In Wordpress the theme is just a 'skin', meaning that you can change your theme at any time and your content will remain intact.

Add an optin box – You will want people to leave their name and email address when they visit your blog. This is accomplished by adding an optin box in the upper right hand corner of your site. You will need an autoresponder service in order to do this. There are several choices for this. Right now I am recommending that you get started with a service called Aweber (my link is http://ConnieLoves.me/Aweber) This includes tutorials and customer service to help you get set up. They also generate the html code you will need, enabling you to simply copy and paste what you need. It's only one dollar for the first month when you sign up using my link, and $19/month thereafter. If you pay quarterly or annually you'll save some money as well.

Step #6 - Create A Free Giveaway

When someone visits your blog, your goal is to interest them enough so they will want to leave their name and email address. The way to do this is by giving them a free gift on your topic. This can be a one page checklist, 10 tips on how to do what you teach, an audio recording, a short video, or a short report. Keep your free gift short and to the point. Remember that this is only to give your prospects a taste of what you have to offer, and to show them that you do have information on your topic that will be valuable to them over time.

What you are reading right now is a short report I put together for those opting in to my newest site. I can then repurpose this content into a variety of different formats, helping people around the globe in the process.

Step #7 - Choose 3 Affiliate Products to Promote

Before I ever had my own product I was promoting affiliate products. This enabled me to see how the process of buying and selling on the Internet really worked, and also gave me some income as I was learning what I needed to do. You can find digital products to sell in a variety of places, including Clickbank and JVZoo. You have also most likely purchased products and courses that you can promote as an affiliate.

On Clickbank – http://Clickbank.com - they will ask you to create a nickname to use for your account. This should be just a short name, using letters and numbers if you like, that will give you your unique name on Clickbank. I recommend not using your name, even though you will mask this link so no one will see it anyway. Clickbank is home to more than 25K digital products, in a wide variety of niches. They will pay you every two weeks once you have met the initial requirements as spelled out in their TOS (terms of service).

Write. Publish. Prosper.

I have found it difficult to find the exact products I need on Clickbank, so I recommend a site called http://ClickbankProSearch.com as a way to search by keyword for what you want to promote to your prospects. This is a paid site, but you can get a 15 day free trial to see how it works. I am there almost every week to find new products to promote and to do my research for new products I will create.

JV Zoo is a newer site that has grown exponentially in the past year. You can not only find products to promote here but also sell your own product through their affiliate program. Take a look at http://ConnieLoves.me/JVZoo to get started.

Now take a look at the products and services you've already purchased online. Most of them will offer an affiliate program, so look for one that fits your niche and sign up as an affiliate. My advice is to only promote three products during your first two or three months of setting up your business. This will keep you focused so you can start making some money and see how this business works. By doing so, you will gain greater insight into how you want to develop your business and what your 'Big Picture' goals will be.

I believe it is important to point out here that you should only promote the products and services you have purchased yourself. You are building your reputation online, and you don't want someone to see that you are promoting their product, service, or training course when you haven't purchased it and benefitted from it yourself. That's the fastest way to lose credibility, and you don't want that to happen. Instead, make the decision to only recommend what you love!

Step #8 - Become a Content Creation Machine

Content creation is at the basis of everything we do online. Whether it be written, spoken, or video our messages must reach our prospects and clients in some format. We typically start writing first, and then move on to audio recordings and videos. Begin by posting to your blog and writing articles regularly. This gives your readers a better idea of who you are and what you stand for. This will take the most time on your part, but it is absolutely crucial to your initial success.

My writing was horrible for the first few months, and it would take me about two hours to write an article or a blog post. Within a couple of months it all got faster and easier, like everything in our life does with practice and now I am able to write and submit an article in about thirty minutes. I use http://EzineArticles.com as my main site to submit my articles. I have been with this site since 2007. You can see how many articles I currently have there by going to my expert bio page at http://ArticlesByConnieRagenGreen.com.

Repurpose your articles into blog posts and short reports. Soon you will find that just one article can be used in many different ways, including turning that content into

Write. Publish. Prosper.

teleseminars and the basis of your own product. Repurposing is the way you can take just one simple idea and turn it into massive content and products of your own.

Host your own teleseminars will jumpstart your business. As soon as possible, let people hear your voice. This makes a huge difference in how quickly you can build your business online. As soon as I started holding a free call every week, more people began to join my list and buy things that I recommended. I want to invite you to hear my latest teleseminar by going to http://AskConnieAnything.com. Sign up for a 21 day trial of the program I've been using for this since 2007 for only $1 at http://TeleseminarStrategies.com

Video is also an excellent way to create content quickly. I still use a Flip camera for all of my videos, but those are no longer made. Instead, go over to Amazon and see the ones you can get for under a hundred dollars at http://ConnieLoves.me/Kodak. I also have my own Channel over at YouTube where you can subscribe at http://YouTube.com/ConnieRagenGreen.

Step #9 - Get Social!

Social media has made it so much easier to get started with an online business than ever before. There was no social media at all during my first year online, and it took another year for it to catch on. You can connect with people who are interested in your topic, and begin to invite them to your blog and to join your list. The 'Big 3' of social media are Twitter, Facebook, and LinkedIn. If you haven't already, go to these sites and claim your name.

Follow me on Twitter by going to http://twitter.com/conniegreen and introduce yourself. Join Facebook and set up your profile. My personal page is at http://facebook.com/ConnieRagenGreen. Join LinkedIn and fill out the information they ask for initially. I'm Connie Ragen Green there as well and you can connect with me at http://www.linkedin.com/in/ConnieRagenGreen. All of these sites will become part of what you do to attract prospects into your business. Just get started now and it will all fall into place over time. Social media can become a huge time waster, so limit yourself to a maximum of thirty minutes a day when you are just starting out, and fifteen to twenty minutes a day as you become more proficient. My motto is 'Get in, get out, and get back to work!' This is also something that can be easily outsourced once you have everything set up initially.

Step #10 – Masterminding and Joint Ventures

My one regret with my own business is that I did not begin connecting your other entrepreneurs much sooner. Instead I stayed home, working at my computer for hours at a time and convincing myself it just wasn't time for me to meet others face to face. Once I took that step in 2008 and began meeting other like-minded individuals my business took off in a huge way. I met people who were both new and filled with great ideas, as well as those who had been working online for ten years already.

Attending live events is the best way to connect with entrepreneurs in person and there are two events I speak at regularly that attract people in every niche you can imagine. One is Dennis Becker's Earn 1K a Day event held each summer, and the best way to get connected with Dennis is by going to http://ConnieLoves.me/WhatHappens and downloading the eBook that chronicles a recent event.

The other event I speak at twice each year is NAMS – the Novice to Advanced Marketing Seminar. You can get started with the free weekly trainings and see how this group could make a difference for you. It's at http://ConnieLoves.me/NAMSWeekly.

I also host my own live events, so if you have joined my list you will hear more about them over time.

I have been provided with many opportunities by attending live events, and would love to meet you in person at one of them.

Step #11 - Your Own Information Products

As soon as you decide that you will stick with your chosen niche for *at least* the next six months, think about a product you will create. You can write a short report, such as I have done here, and sell it for anywhere from $7 to $17. You can then add an audio recording of you reading the report and that could sell for $27. I recommend creating an inexpensive product to begin with, just to understand how the process works. The best training you will receive on how to do this successfully is my comprehensive program at: http://WriteShortReports.com. This is training on a brilliant strategy for creating short report products on your niche topic that your prospects will pay for. Use the code word *PROFIT* to bring it down from the regular price of $37 to only $7.

Remember to keep it simple and include as much detailed information as possible so that you can continue to build your credibility in your niche.

I will recap these eleven steps for you again. They are:

1. Change Your Mindset
2. Choose A Niche
3. Choose A Business Model
4. Purchase Your Domains And Hosting
5. Set Up A Wordpress Blog And Optin
6. Create A Free Giveaway
7. Choose 3 Affiliate Products To Promote
8. Create Content
9. Connect On The 'Big 3' Social Media Sites
10. Connect With Others For Masterminding And Joint Ventures
11. Create Your Own Product

I have oversimplified many things I have included here in this report, but you definitely have enough information to start building your business. The purpose in doing that was to get you to take action quickly without having to think about too many things that can be better addressed down the line. There will be plenty of time to learn the more advanced strategies and techniques of online marketing. For now, just think about going through each of the 11 steps and doing something to start setting the wheels in motion for your future.

Find out more about me and what I am doing at my main site – http://HugeProfitsTinyList.com. You will be able to join my list and also get your free subscription to my popular podcast series.

RESOURCES

I have recommended quite a few excellent resources in this report. Please know that I do not recommend any person, product, or service lightly and that I use and benefit from everything I recommend. Many of these are my affiliate links, meaning that I will receive a commission when you make a purchase. You do not pay any more by going through someone's affiliate link, and many times you are being offered a bonus because of it. This is also one of the best ways for you to start earning money online.

Top 20 WordPress Plugins:
http://TopWPPluginsForBusiness.com

Membership Site Plugin:
http://ConnieLoves.me/Wishlist

My published books:

http://ConnieRagenGreenBooks.com

Autoresponder Services –

http://ConnieLoves.me/Aweber

My link gives you a $1 trial for the first month.

Domains – http://ConnieLoves.me/DomainSale

I purchase all of my domains at GoDaddy because of their excellent customer service and expertise in this area.

Hosting: http://BlueHostSolutions.com

Choose affiliate products: http://Clickbank.com and http://ConnieLoves.me/JVZoo

My published articles:

http://ArticlesByConnieRagenGreen.com

The Earn 1K a Day group:

http://ConnieLoves.me/WhatHappens

NAMS – Novice to Advanced Marketing group:

http://ConnieLoves.me/NAMSWeekly

Create a simple product: http://WriteShortReports.com

Use the code *PROFIT* to bring it down to only $7

Listen to my latest teleseminar at

http://AskConnieAnything.com

Sign up for a 21 day $1 trial to host your own calls at

http://TeleseminarStrategies.com

Inexpensive video cameras:

http://ConnieLoves.me/Kodak

Write. Publish. Prosper.

My Channel on YouTube:
http://YouTube.com/ConnieRagenGreen

DISCLAIMER: I am an affiliate marketer and regularly recommend the products and services I am using in my own online business. I will receive a commission if you purchase these products or services through the links included in this report. I have used or currently continue to use each one I mention here and they each receive my 'Green Seal of Approval'.

To Your Massive Online Success!

Connie Ragen Green

Appendix B

The Writing Process

Writing is an exploration. You start from
nothing and learn as you go.
~ E.L. Doctorow

I have asked two of my colleagues to share something about their own writing process:

From Tim Siglin...

Connie Ragen Green asked me to provide 1,000 words on the writing process I use for technical writing for magazine, website, and electronic newsletter articles. I told her the process was, in essence, all WET.

Not "all wet" in the sense of a damp squib, but WET as an immersive experience to generate quality content for my chosen area of expertise: startups and disruptive technologies in the world of streaming media and digital cinema.

For me the WET acronym—short for Writing, Editing, and Thinking—is as much a state of mind as it is a step-by-step process. Throughout my career, starting with an undergrad in motion picture production and entry into the workforce at the very time that digital video was emerging in the early 1990s, I've been aware that I'm in a highly volatile business.

It's exciting, to be certain, but the rules change on almost a daily basis, as new disruptive technologies force established players to rethink strategies. Take, for example, products and services announced at the 2015 Consumer Electronics Show (CES), to which I'm enroute as I write this chapter.

Three years ago, cable was dominant for premium content delivery to the home, and Netflix was still shipping shiny disks to the majority of Americans. Today "cable cutters" and a generation of "cable nevers" are becoming mainstream. Announcements at CES follow that trend, with major networks and premium content cable channels now available in monthly subscription packages to anyone with decent bandwidth and a smart phone. It's not an ideal viewing experience, especially for premium content purists like myself, but it sure is making life difficult for the average cable monopoly provider in your neighborhood.

Back to WET. Even though it is a great acronym, the T in WET comes first. At the core of my writing process is the thinking surrounding it, whether it be the details of the subject matter itself or the logical argument made about the subject matter.

Thinking needs, nay demands, gestation. Lots of it.

Let me give a personal example of what I mean by this. The first two months of my first job in 1992 were spent researching digital video technologies for the Department of Defense base on which I was part of the contracted public affairs office. As part of that research for our PR team's video and audio deliverables, I read newsgroups—in other words, I read Pine and Gopher text, since newsgroups and web browsers were not quite mainstream—and then called companies and value-added resellers with questions I couldn't get answered online.

I took lots of notes, which led to lots of questions, some of which couldn't be answered without physically trying out the product.

The day came when I had to make a recommendation for two products: one to capture and edit video and one for audio. Let's just say that one recommendation was successful—the audio system was the first version of something called ProTools, which almost every major record album has been recorded on for the last two decades—and the other was a complete flop.

That failure led to significantly more questions, resulting in a list of needs and pain points that would need to be solved to have the ideal digital video solution. I've had that list with me ever since, and every 12-18 months I can check one or two of those technical needs off my list.

That list has been the basis of a career consulting with companies in non-linear editors (think Premiere for your PC) and videoconferencing (think telepresence and telemedicine) and streaming (think Adobe, Microsoft, Real, and many more companies that have made streaming possible). Why? Because it turns out everyone else I talked to had the same pain points, but few of them—including the manufacturers of the products that had potential—had come up with ways to solve the problems the marketplace demanded they solve.

I consistently use the list, and newer lists generated as I moved into streaming technologies about fifteen years ago, to gauge the limitations and opportunities of new digital media and streaming technologies as they enter the market. I'm constantly scanning the horizon for technologies that disrupt or deliver a solution to one of the pain points.

That brings us around to the W in WET, the writing portion.

When a company sends me an emailed press release about their "first ever" product that solves the issue, I can ask very detailed questions about how they're solving the problem—or if they are, since many press releases purport one thing but leave other parts unsaid, for a specific reason. Having been around the industry from its inception, I also tend to retain press releases and technical data from companies, including those that perhaps tried to solve the same problem as a current startup.

When I get a press release today, I often send the older press releases to the new company, asking how their "first ever" approach is different from the technical or business solution from the previous solution that hit the market several years ago. The concepts of "first to market" and "fast follower" aside, the act of presenting a company with a previous iteration of their technology helps me peel back the layers on a press release.

Once I understand how the new technology fits into the overall picture, I then sit down and write. The process of generating 600-1,000 words takes about 45 minutes. It's essentially an explanation of a particular technology and then an argument for or against that technology in light of what the marketplace needs. To provide the best service for my readers, I strive to provide analysis around the press release, allowing them to answer the question "so what?" when it comes to the particular technology. Sometimes that means my articles aren't the first ones to show up on the web, but I'm comfortable that they'll be among the best thought-out articles on any given topic.

That brings us to the final letter in WET.

The E for editing is a two-fold process. First, I edit my own writing as I write, just as I have done with this chapter. That means my first draft is really a second draft.

If the article goes in a magazine, I put it aside for a few days and come back to it to check grammar and logic. Otherwise, I send it to an editor, and rely on him or her to send me back the "so what?" (or WTF, in the case of some of the better editors I've worked with) so that I can think about it and rewrite portions of the article again, strengthening any missing logic the editor caught and also simplifying the wording around a complex concept to make the content more approachable.

Editing is the process that requires a different set of eyes. In fact, it's so important that I'd say the E is the foundation of the whole process. Anyone can write or think about a topic; an editor will think about the content from a logic and grammar standpoint, highlighting areas that aren't clear, or that need further explanation, or cut the crap so that your work sounds better. My wife finished her first novel a few months ago, sent it to an editor, and received back a set of suggestions so powerful that it made the book stand out compared to other books written on the same topic.

An editor is the best money you can spend on any document you write, be it a presentation, an article, a sales pitch, or even a book. I'm happy to make introductions to some of the best editors I know, if you promise to try their services at least once, so that you can see for yourself just how much better your content becomes when a second set of eyes spends quality time with your content.

So that's my process, and it's all WET. I like it that way.

Tim Siglin, Co-founder, Transitions, Inc.
A business and technology development firm and
Chairman, Braintrust Digital, Inc.

© 2015 Braintrust Digital, Inc.
January 8, 2015

From Dennis Becker...

Connie asked me to share with her readers my writing process, and I'm thrilled to be able to contribute to her latest book, even in a small way.

I don't know if I could say that I have a consistent process for writing, certainly not a one-size-fits-all method for sure.

Online, where I tend to hang out most of the time, you've probably heard a gazillion times that content is king. This king wears many different hats... the content might be in the form of a tweet (140 characters or less), making a short comment above a Facebook share, as a forum post, an article, a blog post, some email copy or a sales letter, or a full blown book like Connie's written, and everything in between including this particular "assignment".

Each, at least for me, has a different "writing process" involved... or none at all.

Shorter content involves little or no preparation, you have a thought in your head and you pound it out on your keyboard, being careful to not let auto-correct get in your way.

And then when you press enter, you look at it and say OMG, what did I just do?

That's what I call the Ready, Fire, Aim, method of writing, and for the day to day content, the content that has a limited audience, it's normally good enough.

When I'm preparing something more substantial, again the process will vary.

For a blog post, I often get inspired by a question that someone has asked me recently, and I've already responded to them one on one, and realize that it's something that a wider audience can benefit from.

So in that case, I'll start by copying and pasting the question and answer into my blog post, and then edit it to take out individual references, to make the reply more generic, while still being true to the original message.

There's not much thought involved at all with that method, so really what we're looking at is transforming a human and personal conversation into something more suited for a wider audience, but still maintaining the individuality in the message.

Longer reports and books become more of a challenge because they're less "in the moment" and meant to be better thought out, but what I like to do is break them down.

First I'll brainstorm what problem a reader needs solved, what question they have, or what can I say to them to inspire them.

Sometimes it's just one person who has asked a specific question, and I've internalized it as something that if expanded upon and written about, might be something that a much larger audience might resonate with and hopefully purchase (if for sale) or get to feel better about me, if I'm just trying to get them to know, like, and trust me.

Once I have the general topic in my head, I'll try to attach a title to that topic, something that sounds sort of cool, and something that I would expect they'd answer "yes" to if I said something like "Would you be interested in learning how to eat unlimited chocolate and still lose weight?".

Typically the title in mind has a bit of mystery involved, so that gives me a start on my thought process for phase 2, which is to outline what I want to talk about.

The outline can be done in several ways, and I've done them all...

A basic outline, where you determine your chapter topics. Generally for a typical infoproduct like I tend to write, 10 or 12 chapters is optimal. I recommend the one-problem, one-solution type of book, so we don't want to worry about writing the next great American novel. If you're writing fiction, your results may vary, and you might have dozens of chapters.

Then I'll let that sit for a while, and let my subconscious percolate a bit, maybe a day or two, and while it does that, it will be coming up with ideas for the sub-topics, so when I go back to my master outline and start thinking about each chapter, it will be fairly easy to fill in 8 to 10 talking points for each chapter.

My books tend to be between 15 to 30 thousand words in length, if I plan to market them, or 2 to 5 thousand words if they're meant more for a substantial giveaway report. And of course, for the shorter reports, I'll go with fewer chapters.

Another way of doing a pre-writing outline is to use a mind map. I love this method because it's easy to brainstorm, pointing and clicking and moving things around until they suit my desired end result. Basically it's the same thing as an outline, and still text based, but it's more visual than an outline.

And when I feel more touchy-feely, or need to get away from the computer, I also really like using 3x5 index cards. I have one color that I write my chapter topics onto and another color that I use for the sub-topics.

Using the index cards then, I can move things around very easily, and when I have enough index cards in my hand, like 80 to 120 or so, it just feels so good and substantial.

At that point the writing can start.

So, let's say you have 10 chapters, and on average 10 sub-topics for each chapter. That's obviously 100 things to write about.

If your book is targeted to be around 30,000 words, that means you'll be writing on average 300 words per sub-topic, which is about the same as a short article. If you're familiar with article writing, you might agree that many of them can be knocked off in a very short amount of time, maybe 3 to 5 an hour.

So when you've got to the point of your detailed outline, and start writing that way, the book almost writes itself. Chapter 1, sub-topic 1, write... sub-topic 2, write... sub-topic 3, write... bingo, before you know it, the first chapter is done and on to the next.

There are days when you'll feel like writing and days when you won't. On the days that you don't, you need to push yourself to just do something anyway.

I've always been a big believer in the process of incremental improvement. Every day, in some measurable way, I like to move forward with a project. If my project is writing, I'll set a daily quota of maybe 1000 words, or maybe to write an hour.

Some days you'll feel like busting through that quota and you'll end up with as much as 5000 words written by the end of the day, but it's important to just do something positive to move forward.

If you don't feel like writing, and you get started and still feel like "blah", after you're written about your next scheduled sub-topic or even just 100 words, you'll either have forgotten about the blah feeling and are on track, or you'll realize that you're just not being productive... but you still have those 100 to 300 words in the worst case, and that's worth celebrating.

If you're using the index card type of outline, you can reinforce your progress by putting each card into a file box when that sub-topic is finished. As your book progresses, you then see it visually because at some point there is more in the box than outside waiting to be written, so it becomes a fun competition with yourself to move the cards into the box.

Many writers, myself included, but I admit to having a difficult time with the method, like to postpone all editing until all the writing is done. Doing this gets you into a flow state, getting all your thoughts onto paper without fear of what it looks like.

Sometimes your best thoughts get written that just jump out of nowhere when you write without any worry about editing, knowing that you can change, add, or delete thoughts later.

But once you start to continually stop and correct, you lose your trains of thought, much like you would if you were interrupted by a phone call, or took a break to watch a television show in between paragraphs... not a good idea.

In fact, that's something to force yourself to do when you're in your writing time. Turn off your phone (keep it in another room entirely if at all possible), turn off any instant messengers like Skype, shut down your browser windows so that Facebook doesn't ping at you, and just write.

You want to stay in the flow, get those words on paper, regardless of spelling, regardless of grammar, regardless of whether they make sense at all... and sometimes they won't make sense, trust me on that.

You can edit either of three ways... either you can edit once your chapter is complete, which I recommend, or after each sub-topic is complete (too many stops and starts to my way of thinking, so you lose the flow state), or after the entire book is complete (which might be weeks after you wrote something and you start thinking, why did I write that, what was I thinking?).

Or you can let someone else do your editing for you, but I personally think you should personally edit your original draft, at least once, even if you'll eventually turn it over to someone else for more editing.

So let's break this down. You're writing maybe a relatively substantial 30,000 word book (big enough for almost any one-problem type of book, though perhaps not big enough for a meaty fiction book). You should be able to write this size of a book in a minimum of 30 days, which means 1000 words a day. Most experienced authors can easily write 1000 to 2000 words per day, and at that rate, at worst, if you have 10 to 12 chapters, you'll do each chapter in 2 to 3 days.

Then you can edit that chapter before what you've written gets stale.

And then on to the next chapter, until you're done, which will be sooner than you think.

Many authors swear that they absolutely need and cherish having other people proof read and edit for them.

Do I?

Nope. I do it myself. I go back over what I've written, looking for spelling errors, missing words, confusing style, using the power or a word processor to find and suggest the spelling changes, that kind of thing.

And then I'll usually go through the entire book a third time.

And then after publishing, I'll usually find a spelling error or page 2 or 3. Oops.

So yes, I do recommend that you have other eyes read your book before you publish, but I don't think it's absolutely essential. I've written at length about the "good enough is good enough" theory that I've always had, and I don't personally stress out about a spelling error or two, unless it's in the title...

But if you're known as a notoriously bad speller, or if grammar is a challenge for you, you must... MUST... have someone help you.

Still, I've read plenty of other books that I know were professionally edited at high cost, that still ended up with a few spelling errors, so...

At the end of the day, or the week or the month or however long it takes you to bring your thoughts into print, your amazing new book should be completed and will soon be helping someone, or a lot of somebodies, learn something, solve a problem, or be inspired.

That's why I love to write, and why I think you might also.

Dennis Becker
DennisBeckerCentral.com

Resources

Notable Moments in Self-Publishing History: A Timeline
http://www.pw.org/content/notable_moments_in_selfpublishing_history_a_timeline

The History of Amazon
http://en.wikipedia.org/wiki/Amazon.com

Create Space
https://www.createspace.com/AboutUs.jsp

The History of Amazon Kindle
http://en.wikipedia.org/wiki/Amazon_Kindle

Hosting Your WordPress Blog/Website
http://BlueHostSolutions.com

Hexadecimal Color Charts
http://www.color-hex.com/color-palettes/
http://www.w3schools.com/tags/ref_colorpicker.asp

Teleseminar Service
http://TeleseminarStrategies.com

Website Hosting
http://BlueHostSolutions.com

Affiliate Disclaimer: I am an affiliate for some of the products and services mentioned here and throughout this book. If you should choose to purchase I will receive a commission from the service provider or product creator. Many times I am able to negotiate a better price for you, or additional benefits based on my relationship with them.

About The Author

Connie Ragen Green is a multiple bestselling author of more than ten books, an international speaker, and an award winning small business podcaster.

Formerly as classroom teacher in the public schools of Los Angeles, as well as a real estate broker and certified residential appraiser, Connie left it all behind to start an online business in 2006. She now works with new online entrepreneurs on six continents, helping them to build profitable businesses they can run from their home computers.

Connie has described herself as 'an overnight success that took years to manifest'. She believes that anyone can achieve their dreams and goals if they are willing to do what it takes to make it happen.

Find out more at http://ConnieRagenGreen.com

'Do for a year what others won't;
live the way others can't, forever.'

Made in the USA
Lexington, KY
25 January 2015